author's copy

Simply Delicious
by Orva

Simply Delicious by Orva

*Compiled from the recipes in the first 94 Shows
of the Television Series of the same name.*

Orva Lewis Schultis
with
William Schultis

Copyright © 2002 by Orva Lewis Schultis.

Library of Congress Number: 2002093676
ISBN :	Hardcover	1-4010-6894-4
	Softcover	1-4010-6893-6

All rights reserved. No part of this book may be reproduced or transmitted in any form or by any means, electronic or mechanical, including photocopying, recording, or by any information storage and retrieval system, without permission in writing from the copyright owner.

This book was printed in the United States of America.

To order additional copies of this book, contact:
Xlibris Corporation
1-888-795-4274
www.Xlibris.com
Orders@Xlibris.com
16052-SCHU

Acknowledgements

It is difficult to know just where to start, and even harder to know where to stop in expressing gratitude for all those involved in one way or another in helping get this book into print. First there's Bill Schultis, who "co-produced" the book starting from what was essentially just a stack of recipes. He compiled, organized, rewrote, sketched the illustrations and integrated it all on the data processor. And as part of the bookmaking process there was Shelley Galbraith, whose thorough, even tenacious editing of the manuscript gave me many ideas as well as changes now happily embedded in this volume.

As I developed many of the basic recipes for parties catered by "Parties by Orva", I am indebted to all those who have helped make that an operation to be proud of. Unfortunately, such a list would be far too long. My son Larry and husband Bill helped enormously in setting up my first professional kitchen. Over the course of the years untold numbers of good-natured, hard working staff have made doing parties more fun than going to them.

The television series *"Simply Delicious by Orva"* has been the mechanism by which I have focused my experience through the lens of simplicity to develop the recipes that you see before you. Bill has co-produced that series of shows with me, and at one time or another has served in every capacity. Rick Raunswinder, of Ricks Wine and Gourmet supplied wine for many shows. There have been many members of the staff over the years, including Steve Vlakovich, John Gecan, Karen Fletcher, Camera Operators, Joel Glass, Director for many early shows, Craig Hutchinson, Lighting Engineer, Dick Schwartzbard, Audio Engineer. Steve Vlovich also took many still photographs for our use. Thanks to them all.

About the Authors

Orva Lewis Schultis was born in Illinois and raised in Mississippi. She went to Louisiana State University, where she met Bill, the man soon to be her husband. She received a Bachelor's degree in Economics from Louisiana State University in Baton Rouge just before Bill received his Doctorate in Physics. After teaching for a few years, and having and raising a son, Larry, for a fair few more, she began a career as a caterer.

Orva was owner and head chef of Parties by Orva for more than twenty years. Serving the Washington metropolitan area for all those years, she developed hundreds of recipes, tested at even more events. There are untold numbers of people who have enjoyed her unique approach to food preparation, and loved it!

During those years as a caterer, her husband Bill was building a career at the Institute for Defense Analyses, directing and conducting research, and writing reports on that work for the Department of Defense. He was a member of NATO committees and Chairman of one. This gave Orva and Bill an opportunity to travel in Europe, The United Kingdom, and the Far East. These experiences have broadened Orva's culinary horizons.

In addition to her catering, for the last several years Orva and Bill have co-produced a series of television cooking shows. The series is specifically oriented toward helping very busy couples to get back to home cooking, with recipes that take little time to prepare, and are as good as they remember from their youth. The show is "Simply Delicious by Orva."

Orva and Bill have put this book together from the recipes from the first 94 episodes of Simply Delicious by Orva. The recipes are hers alone.

CONTENTS

INTRODUCTION xvii

SOUP 1
Clear Gazpacho 3
Corn Chowder 4
Creamy Tomato Soup with Basil 5
Quick Shrimp Gumbo 6
Curried Pumpkin Soup 8
Soupe De Poisson Rapide 10
    Easy Rouille 11
Chicken and Dumpling Soup 11
Creamy French Celery Soup 12
French Farm House Creamy Asparagus Soup 13
Cream of Mushroom and Garlic Soup 14
Minestrone Rapide 16
Pistou 17

SALADS 19
Cucumber and Tomato with Basil Vinaigrette 21
    Basil Viniagrette 21
Curried Chicken Salad 22
    Dressing 22
Rice Salad 23
    Dressing for Rice Salad 23
Curried Rice Salad 24
Salsa Salad 25
Green Salad with Bacon 25
Spanish Salad 26
    Viniagrette Dressing 26
Not-Your-Usual Three Bean Salad 27

Beet Salad with Oranges and Walnuts 28
Spiced Beet Salad 29
Roast Beef Salad 29
    Blue Cheese Dressing 30
Chicken Salad with Bacon 30
Cole Slaw Bowl 31
Tuna Salad 32
Vegetable Salad 32
Steak Salad With Green Peppercorn Dressing 33
    Green Peppercorn Salad Dressing 34
Potato Salad 34
Potato Salad with Bacon 35
Roasted Potato Salad with Dijon and Garlic Dressing 36
    Dijon and Garlic Dressing 37
Avocado and Orange Salad 37
Salmon Salad 38
Roast Beef and Tortellini Salad 39
    Creamy Tomato Dressing 39
Warm Chicken and Asparagus Salad 40
Chicken Salad with Pineapple Dressing.....................................41
Caesar Salad 42
    Caesar Salad Dressing 42
Three Vegetable Salad with Balsamic Vinaigrette....................43
    Balsamic Vinaigrette Dressing 43
Cuban Black Bean and Rice Salad...44
Caribbean Shrimp Salad 44
    Mango Sauce 45
Tomato Salad with Feta 45

BEEF 47

Pot Roast with Red Wine 49
Beef Pie 51
Beef and Pasta Sauté 52
Beef and Oyster Pie 53
    Pastry Topping...54
Cottage Pie...54
    Mashed Potatoes 55
Beef Stroganoff 56

Sauerbraten and Dumplings 57
    Dumplings 58
Beef Bolognese 59
Grillades and Grits 60
New Orleans Roast Beef 61
Roast Beef Po Boy 62
Pasta with Roast Beef Sauce 62
Roast Beef Hash 63
Hash Gratin 63
Steak Sandwiches Sublime 64
Creamed Chipped Beef in Vol au Vent Shells.....................65
Sautéed Filets Poivre Vert 66
Garlic and Ginger Beef with Coconut Rice 67
    Coconut Rice 68
Beef with Mushrooms 68
Sesame Beef 70
Beef Curry...70
Beef with Saga Blue and Potatoes 71
Country Beef Pie 72
    Buttermilk Biscuits 72
Bookmaker Sandwich 73
Filet BLT 74

PORK 75
Baked Ham with Bourbon and Brown Sugar Glaze 77
Ham and Cheese Gratin 79
Sautéed Pork Chops 80
Ham and Cheese Rolls 81
Ham and Egg Cobbler 82
Pork Schnitzel 83
    Spaetzele 84
Sweet Potato and Ham Medley 85
Ham and Asparagus Bread Pudding 86
Oriental Pork Burgers 87
    Oriental Pork Burger Sauce 87
Roast Pork Mistral 88
Pork Country Fried Steak 89
    Country Gravy 90

Pork Cutlets "Cordon Bleu" 91
Sausage Po Boy 92
Special Italian Sausage 93
Tex-Mex Frittata 93
Pork Cutlets Saltimbocca 94
Pork Schnitzel With Shallot And Tomato Sauce 95
    Shallot And Tomato Sauce 96

POULTRY 97
Sautéed Goujonettes of Chicken Breast 99
Chicken with Southern Dumplings 100
    Southern Dumplings 101
Quick Cacciatora 102
    Light Tomato Sauce 103
    Fresh Tomato Sauce 103
Breast of Chicken "Cordon Bleu" 104
Dijon Chicken 105
Chicken Breast with Shallots 107
Poulet Mistral 107
Chicken Vol au Vent 109
Easy Repeats 110
Pesto Chicken 110
Chicken Tenders with Stroganoff Sauce 111
Chicken with Oysters 112
Breast of Chicken Stuffed with Stilton 113
Paprika Chicken 114
    Spaetzele 115
Curried Chicken 116
Lime Fried Chicken 117
Chicken and Spaghetti 118
Roast Turkey 119
    Gravy 120
    Fancied-upCranberry Sauce 120
    Basic Conrbread Dressing 121
    Cornbread 122
Turkey Chili 122

SEAFOOD 125

Tuna and Artichoke Pie 127
Salmon Nuggets 128
Simply Delicious Salmon Cakes 129
Dinner Bruschetta 130
Salmon Kedgeree 131
Shrimp Provençal 132
Pesto Prawns 133
Shrimp Aurora 134
Shrimps with Snail Butter 135
Charleston Shrimp 136

EGGS AND CHEESE 137
Chili Con Queso 139
Stacked Cheese Enchiladas 139
Goldenrod Eggs 140
    White Sauce with Cheese 140
Baked Macaroni and Cheese 141
Shrimp Egg Foo Yong 142
    Egg Foo Young Sauce 143
Grilled Swiss Cheese on Sourdough or Rye Bread 143
Quiche with Bacon, Cheese and Green Onion 144

PASTA 145
Pasta with Ham and Spinach 147
Pasta with Creamy Sauce 148
Pasta with Ham and Asparagus 149
Pasta with Asparagus and Snail Butter 150
    Snail Butter 150
French Bistro Macaroni 151
Lemon and Butter Pasta 152
Pasta with Eggplant and Tomato 153
    Pasta Sauce 153
Chicken and Eggplant Pasta 154
Eggplant and Pasta Gratin 155
    To Prepare Eggplant 155
    Arrabbiata Sauce 156
Pasta with Hot Italian Sausage 156
Beef and Saga Blue Pasta 157

Pasta with Beef and Mushrooms 158
Pasta with Hot Italian Sausage and Winter Squash 159
Pasta with Green Peas and Salmon 160
Pad Thai 160
    Prik Nam Pla 162
Fettucini with Fresh Tomato Sauce and Bacon 162

VEGETABLES 163
Quick Sweet and Sour Cabbage 165
Sautéed Potatoes with Rosemary 166
Eggplant 'Napoleons' 167
Savory Sweet 168
Potatoes 168
Green Beans Parmigiana 169
Curried Cabbage 169
Butternut Squash Parmesan 170
Mashed Potatoes 170
Mirleton Gratin 171
Creamed Peas and New Potatoes 172
Braised Cabbage 173
Pumpkin with Parmesan 173
Cooked Fresh Kale 174
Sweet and Sour Cabbage with Orange or Tangerine 174
Grits 175
Coconut Rice 176
Sautéed Red Bliss Potatoes with Almonds 177
Green Beans Amandine 178
Southern "Fried" Corn 178
Sautéed Summer Squash with Onion 179

DRESSINGS AND SAUCES 181
Vinaigrette Dressing 183
Balsamic Vinaigrette Dressing 183
Green Peppercorn Salad Dressing 184
Creamy Tomato Dressing 184
Balsamic Dressing 185
Dijon and Garlic Dressing 185
Caesar Salad Dressing 186

Mango Sauce 186
Marchand de Vin Sauce 187
Light Tomato Sauce 188
Fresh Tomato Sauce 188
Quick Tomato Sauce 189
Shallot And Tomato Sauce 189
Arrabbiata Sauce 190
Turkey Gravy 191
Fancied-up 191
Cranberry Sauce 191
Béchamel Sauce 192
Cumberland Sauce 193
Snail Butter 193
Easy Rouille 194
Country Gravy 194
Prik Nam Pla 195

BREADS AND SUCH 197
Buttermilk Biscuits 199
Black Pepper Biscuits 200
Dumplings 201
Southern Dumplings 201
Basic Cornbread Dressing 202
Cornbread 203
Cheese Cornbread 203
Cheese and Corn Cornbread 204
Patty Cakes 204
Spaetzele 205
Polenta 206
Irish Soda Bread 206
Irish Soda Bread with Cheese and Walnuts 207

DESSERTS 209
All American Dessert 211
Strawberry Fool 211
Southern Ambrosia 212
Banana and Toffee Fool 213
Strawberries with Ricotta 213

Whipped Cream	214
Dessert, Quick and Easy	214
Orange Compote	215
Fruit Salad Dressing	215
Fruit Salad	216
Blushing Fruit Salad	217
Summertime Dessert	218
A Compote Of Strawberries And Apricots	218
Apple Crisp	219
Fried Apples	220
Apple Sauce	220
Profiteroles (Cream Puffs)	221
Georgia Peach Cobbler	222
Apple and Prune Clafouti	223
Blueberry Peach Crumble	224
Sticky Biscuits	225
Apple-Cheese Cobbler	226
Mango Clafouti	227
Blueberry Bread	228
Brownie Cobbler	228
Blueberry Muffins	229
Blueberry and Apple Charlotte	230
Plum and Apple Cobbler	231
Blonde Mincemeat	232
Praline Bananas	232
Plantains for Dessert	233
Baked Apples with Blackberry Jam	234
Peach and Pineapple Cobbler	235
Banana	236
Gingerbread	236
Chocolate Fondue	237
Special Peach Pie	237
Luscious Lemon Pie	239
French Pear Pie	240
Marlboro Pie	241
Pousse Café Tart	241
Lemon Curd	242
Blueberry Sauce	242

Apple Puff	243
Lemon "Pseudo" Ice Box Pie	243
Chocolate Pie	244
Meringues	244
Strawberry Meringue	245
Lemon Blueberry Pie	246
Rubble	247
Pecan Pie	248
Pie Crust	249
Walnut Tart (Flan)	249
Pear and Mincemeat Flan	250
Pineapple Tarts	251
Cheesecake	252
Strawberry Pie	252
Pineapple Puff	253
Apricot Tart	253
Dulce de Leche Tart	254
Banana Cheesecake Tart	245
Upside Down Pudding	246
Lemon Curd	247
Blueberry Sauce	247
Baked Chocolate Filled Pears with Custard	248
Lemon Custard Pudding	249
Zippy Peach Pudding	260
Mama's Bread Pudding	261
Banana Pudding	262
Blueberry Crumble Pudding	262
Caramelized Pineapple with Coconut Custard	263
Strawberry Short Mousse	264
Cheesecake New York Style	265
Upside Down Ginger Pear Cake	266
Coconut Macaroons	267
Chocolate Walnut Cake	268
Mango Meringue Cake	268
Mango Upside-Down Cake	269
Banana Shortcake	270
Blueberry Cheesecake	271
Snow White and Rose Red	272

Quick Cheese Cakes 272
Chocolate Cake 273
Very Chocolate Cake.. 273
Chocolate Ganache Frosting 274
Tropical Ice Cream 275
Chocolate Pie Ice Cream 275
Mango, Strawberry Sundae 276

GLOSSARY 277

INDEX 291

Introduction

There are thousands of cookbooks available to virtually everyone in this country. Shelves of every major bookstore are crowded with cookbooks of all stripes and catering to all tastes. So, why publish yet another?

Many cookbooks focus on a specific cuisine, and others on a region of the country. Still others concentrate on recipes of the great chefs or restaurants of this country or some other. Most recipes are helpful and authentic in their own context. That very authenticity has led to many people viewing cooking as an arcane art fraught with complexities and consuming enormous amounts of time. Indeed much cooking, and therefore many recipes are that way.

After all, most of the cuisines of the world have been developed over centuries, centuries in which cooking occupied much of the time of the cook at home, provided much of the warmth in the home, and perfumed the dwelling with an aroma that gave the feeling of well-being and comfort. As the fire would be lit for the day, why not prepare foods that would simmer slowly and take hours to cook? The cook stove might well be the only source of heat in the home, it would be natural to prepare foods which occupied many hours in the making.

Many of us have been brought up with families eating around the table foods prepared by our grandmothers, or mothers whose job was to make a home with love, cleanliness, and good food. In those circumstances, it seems natural that recipes would be developed without any thought to how long the cooking might take. The more important issues were the cost and availability of ingredients, given the season of the year.

Well, virtually everything has changed, with the possible exception of the time it takes to prepare most recipes that are still being promulgated.

The development and proliferation of refrigeration and transportation early in this century, and the development of many prepared foods and ingredients in the middle to latter part of the century could have had the effect of reducing the time to prepare recipes, but by and large they have not. Neither frozen nor prepared foods have fulfilled their promise of delivering truly delicious meals. They have, however, made available prepared and frozen ingredients that could greatly reduce cooking time, but there have been few attempts to formalize the use of these developments for reassessing and rewriting recipes to take advantage of the existence of these ingredients.

Another great change that has taken place in the last half of the century is demographic. There are far fewer families with stay at home moms, and many more in which both partners work long hours and haven't the time to do much cooking, especially using recipes which were developed without shorter cooking times in mind.

In order to fill this need for delicious dishes that are quick to prepare, I produced a series of television shows called " Simply Delicious by Orva" devoted to the development and exposition of such recipes.

For over 20 years I have been owner and head chef of Parties by Orva, catering events in the greater Washington D.C. Metropolitan area. The television show and the recipes in this book, owe a great deal to the experience I gained in my catering enterprise.

I have always been interested in food, which is not unusual for a child of the South. At home, in Mississippi, fancy food was rare, but basic foods were prepared with love and we made the most of what we had. I spent time in New Orleans in my youth, and surely there are few better places to learn about food and eating. Since that time I have been privileged to travel in Great Britain, the Continent and Korea, always tasting and sampling the wondrous cuisines of the world, learning as I went.

Over the years I have developed many shortcuts without any loss in quality, and the television series has given me a way of sharing my experience with many potential home cooks.

This book is derived from the first 94 shows in that series. The recipes are all thoroughly experimentally verified, as the television crew for those shows will testify, since they were the beneficiaries of the dishes that I prepared on camera.

All of these recipes use only "real", full fat ingredients — butter (not margarine), mayonnaise (unsweetened not "lite" or low fat), real vanilla (not artificial vanilla flavoring), and full fat dairy products — milk, cheese, sour cream and cream cheese, I do not recommend substitutes! Indeed, in many cases substitutes will cause the recipe to fail. In some places I warn again about substitutions, where they can do the most harm to the preparation of the recipe.

I found, in the preparation of this book, that there were places where I could not resist talking directly to you about this or that. I marked those places with a special font (Italics) and with emphasis added that would draw your attention. Some of the recipes are so delicious, for example, that they should get special attention, and I call attention to them with a ***Gourmet Alert!*** Some are so quick that they deserve special attention and they get the ***Timesaver Alert!***. Some are great ways to use leftovers and are labeled, not surprisingly, ***Leftover Alert!***. In some places I have interposed hints or ideas or cooking methodologies that I call to your attention to ***Note!***

Soup

Throughout history, from the Biblical mess of pottage, soup has sustained mankind. It is comforting, economical and nutritious. A delicious soup can be made from a handful of vegetables and herbs.

There is nothing quite so comforting as a bowl of hot soup on a cold and cloudy day. Soup is such a delight, and yet there is so little of it prepared from scratch any more at home, or even in restaurants. Well, nowadays, with a new outlook on cooking illustrated in this book, soup can again become a home-born treasure. The recipes contained in this section, demonstrate that soup can be prepared in a short time and can still be delicious. Big timesavers include precooked products in the supermarket, leftovers properly planned for, and a willingness to prepare "whatever's in the refrigerator soup."

Of course, when you prepare soup, make enough that you can freeze some for another time.

Timesaver Alert! *Note that for any of the soups in this section that call for chicken broth, or any other stock or broth, the canned product can be used. Be careful to get a canned broth that is not seasoned, except by salt. The unflavored ones are tasty and a good, quick substitute for the time consuming process of preparing homemade stock. Major store brands and well-known national brands are quite acceptable. For chicken broth, a good source is your nearby Chinese carry-out. Most sell Won Ton soup. Just ask for that without the Won Ton!*

Clear Gazpacho

Serves 4 to 6
1 quart chicken broth (purchased or homemade)
4 medium tomatoes, chopped
1/3 to 1/2 cup fresh lime juice, to taste
salt
1/2 cup chopped green onions
1 green bell pepper, chopped
2 ribs celery,
chopped fresh coriander (cilantro), optional
sour cream, optional

Pour chicken broth into a large bowl and skim fat. Combine chopped vegetables with broth and salt to taste. Add limejuice to taste. Chill and garnish with fresh coriander and sour cream if desired.

Gourmet & Timesaver Alert! *If you want corn chowder that is quick and as delicious as any you've tasted you've come to the right place. The country ham called for is important—don't substitute the boiled or baked ham from the supermarket. Country ham can be purchased in small pieces or thin slices in your supermarket. Ask where it is if you don't see it.*

*I think I call an alert for nearly every recipe in this section. Just to make it clear, the **_Gourmet Alert!_** denotes a recipe that is truly a gourmet item; the **_Timesaver Alert!_**, one that is very quick to prepare. Often recipes in this book are both.*

Corn Chowder

Serves 4
4 ounces diced country ham
1 medium onion, diced
1 small rib celery, diced
2 to 3 medium potatoes, diced
2 tablespoons butter
2 cans (15 ounce each) creamed corn
2 cups water
1 can (12 ounce) evaporated milk
salt and pepper to taste

In a heavy, 2-quart pan with a lid, gently sauté the ham in the butter for 2 to 3 minutes. Remove ham and sauté the raw vegetables until wilted and just beginning to color. Add water and cover and simmer for about 15 minutes or until the vegetables are tender. Add corn and milk and bring almost to a boil. Add ham and simmer for about 5 minutes. Season to taste at this point.

Timesaver Alert! *It doesn't get quicker, or for that matter better than this. On a cold evening, come home from work and in less than half an hour you've got a delightful supper of soup (add a salad from the next section for a complete meal)*

Note! *Pesto, used in the following recipe, is a sauce for pasta or for flavoring in soup. The classic version is composed of basil, olive oil, Parmesan or Romano cheese, and pine nuts or walnuts worked into a paste. Many brands of refrigerated commercial pesto are quite acceptable.*

Creamy Tomato Soup with Basil

Serves 4
1 small onion, diced
3 tablespoons butter
2 tablespoons all-purpose flour
1 can (28 ounce) plain tomatoes (salt only)
2 heaping teaspoons basil pesto (to taste)
salt to taste
chicken broth if desired

Melt butter and cook onion until soft then stir in flour, cooking and stirring for about 2 minutes. Add the entire can of tomatoes and cook until hot, about 5 minutes. Purée soup and return to heat. Season with pesto, stir, and season to taste with salt. If soup is too thick, thin with chicken broth or water to the desired consistency

Gourmet Alert! *It is an unfortunate fact that not everyone lives in or near New Orleans. There are many of us who do not have ready access to numerous restaurants that serve delightful gumbo. Very few of us have time or inclination to make gumbo the old fashioned way. This is as good a gumbo as I've ever had and does not take all day as soups and gumbos used to do before the new way of cooking introduced in this book. Don't be frightened off by the okra. It gives the gumbo body, and a deep, rich flavor. If you've never tried gumbo you're in for a treat. Just try it and you'll be sold.*

Quick Shrimp Gumbo

Serves 6 for starters, 4 for meal
1 medium onion, diced
1 teaspoon chopped garlic (use purchased in a jar for convenience)
few sprigs parsley, chopped
3 tablespoons vegetable (not olive) oil
3 tablespoons flour
4 ounces country ham, chopped
2 tablespoons butter
1 pound raw shrimp, peeled, save peels
1/2 bell pepper, optional
1 can (28 ounce) chopped tomatoes in juice (unflavored)
1 can (10 1/2 ounce) chicken broth
1 box (12 ounce) frozen sliced okra, thawed (1 pound of fresh okra, trimmed and sliced, may be substituted)
hot sauce to taste

Place the reserved shrimp shells in a small pan and pour chicken broth over them, simmer over low heat. While the broth is simmering, start the gumbo. In a small skillet, combine oil and flour and over low heat, cook stirring frequently until the roux is a rich chestnut brown. NOTE: CAUTION — IT BURNS VERY EASILY!

While the roux is browning, melt butter in a heavy non-reactive pot (avoid aluminum or copper), preferably one that can go to table. Sauté onion, garlic, parsley, pepper, okra and ham. Cook until okra no longer "ropes."* When the vegetables are well softened, strain the broth over and discard the shrimp shells, simmer gently. When roux has reached the desired color, add carefully to the other ingredients. NOTE: CAUTION — IT WILL SPLATTER. Stir to blend. Bring gumbo to a gentle boil, to allow roux to thicken soup. Add shrimp and simmer until they curl and turn pink, about 3 minutes. Season to taste with salt and black pepper. Serve with rice cooked according to packet directions.

* Ropes: Okra gives off strings of thick liquid as it cooks. When it stops doing this, it is cooked.

<u>Note!</u> *Roux: A mixture of equal parts fat (oil, butter, or lard) and flour cooked very slowly until it reaches a rich brown color. It is used as a thickening agent for soups and sauces. It is the basis for most traditional Louisiana dishes. It adds flavor and richness to sauces and prevents the formation of lumps that are inevitable if flour is added directly to a sauce.*

Roux can be made in quantity, and kept refrigerated almost indefinitely in a tightly closed container.

Curried Pumpkin Soup

Serves 6
1 medium onion, finely diced
1 tablespoon butter
2 cans (about 1 pound each) pumpkin
1 can (10 1/2 ounce) chicken broth
2 1/2 cups whole milk
2 teaspoons curry powder or to taste
1/2 teaspoon coarse granulated garlic
juice 1/2 lemon
salt to taste

In a 2-quart pot over medium heat, sauté onion in butter until soft and add curry powder and cook for about 1 minute. Then add pumpkin and broth and heat, whisking together. Add milk in three parts, stirring in thoroughly after each addition. When soup is at serving temperature and thinned to your taste, add the lemon juice, garlic powder and then salt to taste.

Gourmet Alert! It has been my pleasure to visit Paris, and I fell in love with Soupe de Poisson. I love the taste, and the way it was served, with the dishes of cheese, rouille, and croustades accompanying the soup. I ate it at almost every meal. (Well, not at breakfast!) When I returned home I missed it terribly, so I started to experiment. We have different kinds of fish available in this country. We find it difficult to buy fish heads and carcasses to make stock, but I persevered and found that commercial clam juice makes an acceptable substitute. If you try it, also try the Rouille. It is added to the soup just before or at the table. First try a little, then you'll know how much more to put in.

Note! The recipe for rouille is given just after the soup recipe. Rouille is easy to make and by using commercial mayonnaise as the base can be made up very quickly and is safer than one made with raw egg. It's just as good made this way!

Note! Mayonnaise: I recommend purchased mayonnaise, primarily because mayonnaise made from scratch requires the use of raw eggs, which can be dangerous nowadays, and takes way too long to prepare. I recommend unsweetened mayonnaise for all uses. The formula for mayonnaise is eggs, oil, lemon juice or vinegar and salt. Commercial mayonnaise contains those items, but many brands also contain sweeteners and additives. There are a few brands, Duke's for example, that contain the basics and nothing else. Sugar is undesirable for most salad dressings, and you should decide which and how much.

Soupe De Poisson Rapide

Serves 6 for starters or 4 for meal
2 bottles (6 1/2 ounce each) clam juice
2 tablespoons extra virgin olive oil
1 medium to large onion, finely chopped
1/4 cup parsley, finely chopped
1 large ripe tomato, diced or 1 cup unseasoned canned tomato
1 pound raw shrimp, shelled and shells reserved
1/2 pound white fish, i.e., cod, haddock, etc., in 1/2 inch dice
1 cup water
salt and pepper to taste
Easy Rouille (recipe follows)
shredded Parmesan cheese
toasted French bread rounds (croustades)

In a small pan cover the shrimp shells with the water and bring to a boil and simmer while proceeding. In a heavy 2-quart saucepan sauté onion and parsley in olive oil until soft then add tomato and cook until juices flow. Add clam juice, shrimp and fish and cook until seafood is cooked (about 5 minutes). Strain and add broth from shrimp shells. Purée the soup, either in a food processor or with a hand held blender. Reheat soup and season to taste, it will take rather a lot of salt. Serve in soup plates with a toasted round of French bread, rouille to taste and shredded Parmesan cheese.

Easy Rouille

1 cup mayonnaise (containing no sugar) do not use low fat
1 teaspoon finely minced garlic
a generous pinch paprika
salt to taste
Blend all ingredients together and refrigerate.

Chicken and Dumpling Soup

Serves 4 generously
1 quart chicken broth (three 10 ounce cans will work)
1 small onion, diced
1 rib celery, diced
1 tablespoon butter
Dumplings Include:
1/2 cup self-rising corn meal
1/2 cup self-rising flour
1 large egg
1 tablespoon vegetable oil
1/4 cup, approximately, milk

In a heavy 3-quart pan with a lid, melt the butter and gently sauté the onion and celery until they wilt and soften. Then add broth and bring to a boil. Reduce heat to a simmer. Make dumplings by combining the corn meal and flour and adding the egg and oil. Add milk a bit at a time stirring until ingredients are mixed thoroughly. The resulting dough should not be sloppy, but just moistened enough to stick together. Make dumplings about the size of a cherry tomato and add them to the simmering broth. Put lid on pan and simmer for about 10 minutes until dumplings are cooked through. (Cut one open to check for doneness.)

Creamy French Celery Soup

Serves 6
3 tablespoons extra virgin olive oil
3 tablespoons all-purpose flour
3 cans (10 1/2 ounce each) chicken broth and enough water to make 6 cups
1 large bunch celery, taken apart and washed thoroughly
1 bunch green onions
salt and pepper to taste
Easy Rouille (see page 11)
grated Parmesan cheese, if desired

In a heavy 3 to 4 quart pan with lid, heat the olive oil slightly and whisk in the flour. When well blended, add the liquid and whisk to blend. Cut the celery branches into crosswise slices an inch or so wide and add to the pan. Wash and slice the green onions, white and green parts into similar lengths. Cover and simmer for about 30 minutes or until very tender. Purée the soup. Season to taste. Serve hot with a dollop of rouille and a sprinkle of cheese, if desired.

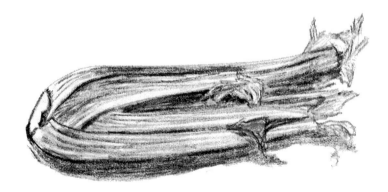

French Farm House Creamy Asparagus Soup

Serves 6
3 tablespoons olive oil
3 tablespoons all-purpose flour
Two cans (10 1/2 ounce each) chicken broth and 1 cup water
3 pounds asparagus, washed thoroughly
1 bunch green onions
salt and pepper to taste
easy rouille (see page 11)
grated Parmesan cheese, if desired

In a heavy 3 to 4-quart pan with lid, heat the olive oil slightly and whisk in the flour. When well blended, add the liquid and whisk to blend. Break off the tough ends and cut the asparagus stalks into slices an inch or so long and add to the pan. Wash and slice the green onions, including white and green parts, into similar lengths and add them to the pan. Cover and simmer for about 30 minutes or until very tender. Purée the soup. Season to taste. If the soup seems too thick, thin with a small bit of water or broth. Serve hot with a dollop of rouille and a sprinkle of cheese, if desired.

Cream of Mushroom and Garlic Soup

Serves 6

3 green onions, rinsed and cut into 1/2 inch pieces
1 small onion, peeled and sliced
2 heads of garlic
1 pound mushrooms, rinsed and cut into quarters
4 tablespoons butter
4 tablespoons flour
1 can (10 1/2 ounce) chicken broth
2/3 cup milk
1/3 cup cream or half & half
salt and pepper to taste

Divide the garlic into cloves and simmer in boiling water for about 1 minute (this will loosen the skin). Remove from water. Let garlic cool and then peel and set aside. Melt the butter over low heat in a heavy 3-quart pot with a lid and simmer the mushrooms and onions, covered, for about 5 minutes or until the vegetables are wilted and the mushrooms have given off considerable juice. Remove the vegetables from the pan and reserve while sautéing the flour in the butter and juice for about 2 minutes. Stir until all lumps are dissolved. Slowly stir in the broth and whisk until smooth. Return the mushrooms and onion to the pot and also add the garlic. Simmer gently for about one hour until the garlic is meltingly soft. Purée the soup and stir in the milk and cream. Bring back to serving temperature and season to taste. A small dollop of sour cream or a sprinkle of finely chopped parsley is attractive.

Note! To select fresh garlic, choose bulbs that are heavy for their size. The cloves should be plump, and firm, and unbruised. They can be stored for only a week or two, because they start to dry up. For most of the recipes in this book, it is not necessary to use fresh garlic; indeed I suggest otherwise. Jars of finely chopped or puréed fresh garlic or dry granulated garlic are readily available, and quite good. The chopped or puréed must be refrigerated after opening.

Note! Mushrooms for soup can be pristine and firm, or ones that have begun to age or darken. Soup is a good way to use mushrooms that are past their prime, but have not yet begun to spoil, because mushrooms intensify in flavor as they age. If you are doing stuffed mushrooms for a party, Cream of Mushroom and Garlic Soup is a good way to use up the stems.

Minestrone Rapide

Serves 6

1 can (15 ounce) of Cannellini or Great Northern beans
1 can (28 ounce) diced tomatoes in juice
4 ounces bacon or country ham, diced
2 celery stalks
2 large carrots
1 bunch green onions
1 small onion
2 tablespoons purchased pesto or to taste
2 tablespoons chopped garlic
1 or 2 cans (15 ounce each) chicken or vegetable broth
4 ounces kale, approximately, sliced
2 zucchini or summer squash
freshly grated or shredded Parmesan or Romano cheese

In a heavy, non-reactive (not aluminum or copper) 3-quart pot fry the bacon and ham, without adding additional fat until it begins to render. Chop carrots, celery, green onions, and onion very finely in a food processor or by hand and add to the pot with the garlic and canned tomato and one can of broth. Cover and on high heat, bring to a boil and then reduce heat and simmer for about 30 minutes until vegetables are tender. Add drained and rinsed beans, shredded greens and squash and simmer, uncovered, for about 15 minutes. If soup is too thick, add the other can of broth and heat. Add pesto and stir to mix then add salt and pepper to taste. Pass cheese with soup to be added at table.

Pistou

1 package (1 pound) julienne vegetables (a mix of broccoli, cauliflower, cabbage and carrot) or make your own
1 small onion, diced
1 rib celery, diced
1 tablespoon extra virgin olive oil
1 quart chicken broth, approximately (three 10 1/2 ounce cans plus a little water)
1/2 teaspoon garlic purée
a few sprigs parsley
purchased basil pesto
Easy Rouille (see page 11)

In a 3-quart heavy saucepan, sauté the onion and celery in the olive oil. When they have started to soften, add the mixed vegetables and the broth. Bring to a boil and reduce heat to a simmer. Cook for about 10 minutes and then season to taste with salt and pepper. Add garlic. Don't add too much, as the rouille has garlic in it as well. To serve, ladle into bowls and season to individual tastes with pesto and rouille.

Salads

Lettuces were very popular with the early Romans. At that time they were served at the end of the meal to induce sleep. Later they gravitated to the beginning to stimulate the appetite. By this time salads were similar to their present form, served with a dressing. After the Roman Empire fell, so did the salad, not to reappear until the Middle Ages, when lettuce was mentioned by Chaucer. From that time on salads were increasingly popular in England and later in the colonies. Some other familiar salad ingredients such as radishes, onions and garlic were used by the Egyptians and are mentioned in the Bible.

Contributing to the popularity of lettuce and other salad ingredients in former times was their cold tolerance. They could be harvested in early spring and winter when other fresh produce was unavailable, and people were starved for anything fresh.

I can well remember, when I was a child, how eagerly my family greeted the early arrival of salad fixin's.

Salads, unlike soups, have become very popular because they are viewed as easy and quick to prepare, and healthful as well. Salads can be as simple as lettuce with a dressing, or can be an entire meal. The whole spectrum is represented in this collection.

Of course, one of the principal elements of a good salad is it's dressing. A wide variety of dressings is presented, including a variation of Caesar Dressing that does not use raw eggs, which can be rather dangerous nowadays.

Cucumber and Tomato with Basil Vinaigrette

Serves 4
2 to 3 tomatoes, about 1 pound
1 European cucumber
1 medium size sweet onion
1 bell pepper, optional (yellow or orange would add color)

Dice all vegetables (about 1/4 inch) and combine them. Toss with dressing and, if possible, allow to sit for 20 or 30 minutes before serving.

Basil Vinaigrette

3/4 cup mix of olive and vegetable oils, to taste,
(about 1/2 cup extra virgin olive and 1/4 cup vegetable)
1/4 cup wine vinegar
1 heaping teaspoon basil pesto (purchased is fine) or
1 tablespoon fresh basil, finely chopped
1 teaspoon salt

Combine all ingredients and shake or whisk together thoroughly. Refrigerate any leftover dressing.

Gourmet Alert! *Here's a salad that's a complete meal. The walnuts and celery provide the crunch, and the chicken the protein. Try the dressing just as it is the first time. After that make your own variations.*

Note! *When you do make your own variations it would be helpful to realize that when using curry powder both a sweet component and an acid one are necessary to balance the curry. Here the juice supplies both: raisins supply additional sweetness, and pineapple the acidity.*

Curried Chicken Salad

Serves 4 (you'll have leftovers)
3 cups diced cooked chicken, skin and bones
1 1/2 cups diced celery, cut smaller than the chicken
1 cup walnuts
1/2 cup golden raisins

Combine the above ingredients and toss together, then toss with the following dressing.

Dressing

1 1/2 cups mayonnaise
1/4 cup orange or pineapple juice
2 teaspoons curry powder
salt to taste

Combine ingredients and whisk together thoroughly then combine with chicken salad ingredients above.

Rice Salad

Serves 6
4 cups cooked rice
(use converted rice and follow the directions on the box)
1 orange
1 cup sliced grapes or diced, unpeeled apple
1 cup canned diced pineapple
1 teaspoon cinnamon greens

Toss all ingredients thoroughly and then toss with dressing. Using warm rice is best because it absorbs the dressing better, but cold leftover rice will work quite well too. After dressing the salad, taste and if needed, add salt and/or sugar. Serve on a bed of greens.

Dressing for Rice Salad

1/2 cup vegetable oil
2 tablespoons wine or fruit vinegar
1/4 teaspoon salt
1 tablespoons granulated sugar

Mix or shake all ingredients together until salt and sugar are dissolved. Toss with rice mixture.

Curried Rice Salad

Same as Rice salad with the addition of
2 teaspoons curry powder added to dressing
1/2 cup walnuts or almonds or pinenuts.

<u>Timesaver Alert!</u> Here's an old standby with a new twist. Get the cabbage already shredded from the supermarket and save the cutting time. This goes well as a side dish or light salad. It's a must with barbeque.

Cole Slaw

Serves 4
4 cups finely sliced cabbage
or 1 package slaw mix from grocery
Dressing
1/2 cup mayonnaise
1/4 cup buttermilk or sour cream
2 tablespoons wine vinegar
1 teaspoon celery seed
1 teaspoon salt

Thoroughly mix dressing ingredients and toss with cabbage. If possible allow to sit for about half an hour before serving.

Salsa Salad

Serves 4
1 pound tomatoes
1 green or yellow bell pepper
1 medium size sliced onion
1 avocado (optional)
1/4 cup fresh lime juice
2 tablespoons fresh coriander (cilantro)

Dice vegetables, about 1/4 inch, and combine in a salad bowl, preferably glass because the salad colors are pretty. Toss vegetables with limejuice and coriander. Salt to taste.

Green Salad with Bacon

Serves 4-6
allow 1 cup greens (romaine or leaf lettuce) per person
1/4 pound bacon, diced before frying
Vinaigrette Dressing (See page 26)

Fry bacon until crisp , remove from fat and drain on paper towels. Wash greens and tear into bite-size pieces if necessary. Drain thoroughly. Place greens in salad bowl and pour dressing over, use only as much dressing as necessary. Don't drown the salad. Sprinkle bacon bits on top.

Spanish Salad

Serves 4-6

1 large or 2 small cans (6 1/2 ounce each) solid pack tuna in oil, drained
1 pound flavorful tomatoes, cut in bite-size pieces
1 red bell pepper, roasted and skinned (see note),
or 1 medium jar pimento (about 3 ounces)
1 pound new potatoes cooked until done but still firm, cut in bite-size pieces
mesclun or romaine lettuce, about 2 cupfuls
1 pound vegetable of choice (broccoli or asparagus), blanched (see notes below)

Place greens on bottom of tray or flat dish and build up salad by layers. Start the layers with potatoes, then tomatoes, then green vegetables, then tuna and top with pepper or pimento. Pour Vinaigrette Dressing over just before serving.

Vinaigrette Dressing

3/4 cup extra virgin olive oil
1/4 cup wine vinegar
salt and pepper to taste

Place all ingredients in jar with cover and shake well before using.

Note! *To Skin Tomatoes: Drop whole tomatoes into a pot of boiling water and remove in about 1 minute into a bowl of cold or ice water. As soon as they are cool enough to handle remove skins and use as desired.*

<u>Note</u>! *To Blanch Vegetables: Cut vegetables into bite-size pieces. Drop the vegetables of choice into a generous amount of rapidly boiling water (the amount depends on the amount to be blanched). Allow to remain in water about 2 minutes then remove vegetables to large bowl filled with cold or ice water to chill rapidly. This tenderizes and sets color of vegetables.*

<u>Note</u>! *To Roast Peppers: Place washed pepper(s) in unsealed plastic bag and place into microwave and cook on high heat for 5-10 minutes depending on the power of the microwave. The peppers should be thoroughly wilted. When they reach this point, remove from microwave, still in bag, being very careful because they will be very hot. Allow to cool in bag. The skins should remove with ease.*

Not-Your-Usual Three Bean Salad

Serves 6 to 8
1 each, approximately 1 pound cans, of white, red and black beans
1/2 cup celery, diced
1/2 cup onion, diced
1 tablespoon chopped parsley

Drain beans and rinse thoroughly. Combine beans with all other ingredients and toss with an olive oil based vinaigrette (see preceding page). Chill thoroughly. This salad is especially good if made the day before and refrigerated.

<u>Note</u>! Beets are so good in salad, and walnuts go so well with them that I believe the next two recipes might become favorites.

Beet Salad with Oranges and Walnuts

Serves 6

2 cans (approximately 1 pound each) plain sliced beets, drained
grated zest of 1/2 orange
2 oranges, peeled and sliced crosswise
1/4 cup chopped walnuts
2 tablespoons extra virgin olive oil
2 teaspoons balsamic vinegar
pinch of cinnamon
1/2 teaspoon salt
1 teaspoon sugar

Heat olive oil in skillet and cook beets for 2 to 3 minutes. Add orange zest, pinch of cinnamon, balsamic vinegar, salt and sugar. Raise heat and cook until liquid is almost absorbed. Add walnuts and turn into serving dish. Immediately before serving add orange slices. They cannot be added earlier because they will absorb color from the beets and the contrast will be lost.

Spiced Beet Salad

Serves 4
1 can spiced beets
1 green onion, sliced thinly
1/4 cup broken walnut pieces
1 tablespoon extra virgin olive oil

Combine all ingredients and garnish with parsley or other green and serve.

Gourmet & Leftover Alert! *This is a great way to use leftover roast beef. Don't leave out the blue cheese, it's what gives this dish its distinctive flavor.*

Roast Beef Salad

Serves 4
1 pound medium rare roast beef, cut into bite-size chunks
1 pound Red Bliss potatoes cooked just until easily pierced by knife
3 to 4 green onions, washed and sliced
Blue Cheese Dressing (homemade or purchased)

Cool, peel and cut the potatoes into chunks about the same size as the pieces of beef and add the green onion. Toss with the blue cheese dressing and pile onto a bed of crisp lettuce leaves.

See Blue Cheese Dressing on the next page.

Blue Cheese Dressing

1/4 pound blue cheese, crumbled
1 cup mayonnaise
1/2 cup buttermilk
1 teaspoon horseradish

Combine all ingredients well and stir as needed into salad. Don't use too much. Refrigerate unused dressing and it will last almost indefinitely.

Timesaver Alert! *To save time you can use roast chicken that you get from your local supermarket for this salad, or use leftovers of your own roast chicken. If you plan a week's meals ahead, you can save a lot of time and never have leftovers that look and taste like leftovers.*

Chicken Salad with Bacon

Serves 6 to 8
3 pounds boneless, skinless chicken breast, cooked and diced
1/2 pound bacon, cooked, crumbled and drained
3 ribs celery, diced
1/4 cup dill pickle relish, or chopped dill or sour pickles
1 cup mayonnaise
1 medium tomato
salt and few dashes of Tabasco

In a large bowl combine chicken, bacon, celery and pickle. Purée tomato and stir into mayonnaise. Add Tabasco to taste. Toss with the other ingredients, adding more mayonnaise if necessary to make a well dressed, but not soupy salad. Add salt to taste. Refrigerate.

Note! _Try this when you have folks over for a light supper or barbecue. The cabbage itself forms the bowl that the slaw is served in. It looks great and takes very little time._

Cole Slaw Bowl

Serves 6
1 large cabbage
1/2 cup mayonnaise
1/4 cup buttermilk
1 teaspoon celery seed
2 teaspoons vinegar
salt and pepper

Rinse cabbage, removing any damaged leaves. Cut off 1/3 of the cabbage (Stem end) leaving 2/3 cabbage to form the bowl. Scoop out bowl with a short heavy pairing knife, reserving the removed cabbage for the slaw. Hollow out the bowl so that the walls are about 1/2–3/4 inch thick. Set bowl aside.

Use all cabbage except the bowl and the core, to make the slaw. Chop finely. In a large kitchen bowl, combine mayonnaise, buttermilk, celery seed and vinegar. Whisk until smooth. Salt and pepper to taste. Stir in chopped cabbage. Stir to blend with sauce. With a slotted spoon, separate slaw from excess liquid, and fill the cabbage bowl. Bowl can be reused later, if it is refrigerated after use, as a vegetable or to make slaw.

Tuna Salad

Serves 4

2 cans (6 1/2 ounce each) tuna in oil, drained
1 can (approximately 1 pound) red beans, drained and rinsed
2 ribs celery, sliced
2-3 green onions, sliced
1/4 cup sliced green olives
1/2 cup extra virgin olive oil
lemon juice
leaf lettuce for bed

Combine all ingredients and toss. Serve on a bed of leaf lettuce.

Vegetable Salad

Serves 6

1 can (approximately 1 pound) black-eye peas, drained and rinsed
1 can (approximately 1 pound) sliced beets, drained
2 ribs celery, sliced
2-3 green onions, sliced
1/2 cup extra virgin olive oil
approximately 2 tablespoons vinegar
leaf lettuce

Combine all ingredients and toss. Serve on a bed of leaf lettuce.

Steak Salad With Green Peppercorn Dressing

Serves 1
4 ounces beef filet steak, cut into bite-size pieces
2 tablespoons butter
2 to 3 cups mesclun or torn leaf lettuce
about 4 slices Portabello mushrooms or 2 medium regular mushrooms, sliced
1 ounce crumbled Roquefort cheese
1 medium tomato, cut into bite-size pieces
1/2 cup purchased shoestring potatoes (from a can)
2 tablespoons purchased fried onions (from a can)
dressing

Heat butter until it sizzles then sauté mushrooms and steak, use a large enough skillet so they aren't crowded (if they are crowded, they steam). When cooked to desired doneness, remove from skillet and set aside. On a dinner plate, make a nice mound of washed mesclun or lettuce and arrange tomato over. Drizzle with dressing (next page) and sprinkle potatoes around lettuce to make a border and sprinkle onions over top of salad. Serve immediately.

Green Peppercorn Salad Dressing

1 cup vegetable oil
1/3 cup wine vinegar
2 teaspoons salt
1 heaping tablespoon Dijon mustard
2 teaspoons brine packed green peppercorns, drained and crushed

Combine all ingredients and whisk vigorously until well blended. This dressing improves if allowed to blend refrigerated, for 24 hours. The brine packed green peppercorns can be purchased at oriental markets and if kept refrigerated in their liquid in a tightly closed jar will keep indefinitely.

Potato Salad

Serves 4 to 6
2 pounds, approximately, salad potatoes such as Red Bliss
1 cup mayonnaise or sour cream or a mix of 1/2 cup of each
3 tablespoons grainy mustard
1 tablespoon Dijon mustard
1 tablespoon wine vinegar
salt and pepper to taste
2 green onions, finely chopped
paprika for color

Scrub the potatoes well and only peel if skins look ragged. Leave new potatoes whole. Cut large potatoes into uniform pieces about the size of an egg. Place potatoes in sauce pan which has a lid and which is large enough to hold the potatoes without crowding. Cover with water and add 1 teaspoon salt and cover. Cover pan and bring to a boil. Turn down heat and simmer about 15 minutes or as needed to cook potatoes until just tender but still firm. Test by sticking a potato with a sharp paring knife. When done the knife should slide into the potato smoothly. Remove potatoes from water and allow to cool thoroughly in a plate or dish lined with paper towels. Potatoes may be cooked the day before and refrigerated covered until needed.

Mix the mayonnaise and/or sour cream with the mustards, vinegar and salt and pepper. Toss with the potatoes as needed, any leftovers dressing can be refrigerated and used in another salad. Just before serving, sprinkle the salad with the chopped green onion and paprika for color

Potato Salad with Bacon

Serves 6

1 1/2 or 2 pounds small new Red Bliss potatoes
1/2 pound thick sliced bacon, cut into cubes
1 medium head Romaine lettuce, washed
1 rib celery, washed
1 medium tomato, washed

Dressing Ingredients

1/2 cup extra virgin olive oil
1/2 cup vegetable oil
1/4 cup red wine vinegar
2 tablespoons Dijon mustard
salt and pepper to taste

Wash and cook the potatoes until they are done but still quite firm. Cut the bacon into 1 inch pieces and fry until crisp and drain on paper towels. Cut the potatoes into large bite-size pieces and place into serving bowl. Slice in the celery and romaine and coarsely dice in the tomato then add the bacon. Mix the salad dressing until well blended and pour half of it over the salad and toss gently. Use more dressing if desired. Refrigerate remaining dressing.

Roasted Potato Salad with Dijon and Garlic Dressing

Serves 4 to 6
2 pounds Red Bliss potatoes, washed
dressing
Preheat oven to 350°F

If using small new potatoes cut them in half; cut larger potatoes into 1-inch cubes. Do not peel potatoes unless necessary. Toss with roughly one half the dressing (next page), being sure potatoes are thoroughly coated, and place in a baking pan. Cover with aluminum foil and bake for about 1 hour, or until they are tender but not soft. Remove the foil and turn the potatoes; then continue roasting until they are well browned. Before serving, toss potatoes with just enough dressing to cover very lightly.

Dijon and Garlic Dressing

1 cup vegetable oil
1/4 cup cider or wine vinegar
1/2 cup Dijon mustard
2 tablespoons garlic purée
1 1/2 teaspoons salt

Combine all ingredients and process or beat until thoroughly emulsified. Refrigerate any unused portion.

Avocado and Orange Salad

Serves 1
1/2 avocado, sliced
1/2 orange lime
salt to taste
greens for lining dish

Peel and slice avocado. Peel the orange with a knife, slicing off all the pith and slice crosswise, not into segments. Arrange over a bed of greens and squeeze lime over.

Salmon Salad

Serves 4

12 ounces, approximately, cooked fresh salmon
1 can (19 ounce) Cannelloni or Great Northern beans
1/2 of a long European cucumber, cut into chunky wedges
2 plum tomatoes, cut into wedges
3 green onions, sliced into 1/4 inch pieces
3 to 4 crisp radishes, cut into wedges
the leaves from several sprigs
fresh thyme
4 sprigs fresh cilantro, chopped
few sprigs parsley chopped
1/2 cup extra virgin olive oil
juice and grated zest of 2 lemons
salt and pepper to taste
lettuce leaves for bed

In a bowl, large enough to hold all the ingredients, whisk together the olive oil and lemon. Crumble in the salmon and add the remaining ingredients and toss together. Taste for seasoning and add salt and pepper to taste. Serve on bed of lettuce.

Roast Beef and Tortellini Salad

Serves 6
2 cups (about) roast beef cut into bite-size pieces
4 cups cooked and chilled cheese tortellini
1 large rib celery, diced
1 medium tomato, diced
Creamy Tomato Dressing
greens

Combine first 3 ingredients and set aside while making dressing. Add dressing and toss gently so as to not break pasta. Serve on bed of lettuce.

Creamy Tomato Dressing

1 cup mayonnaise
1 medium tomato, puréed
2 tablespoons Crystal hot sauce
salt to taste

Purée tomatoes and mix thoroughly with the mayonnaise. Add hot sauce and stir to mix. Season to taste. Also good on chicken salad.

Warm Chicken and Asparagus Salad

Serves 4
1 bunch asparagus, about 1 pound
1/2 pound breast of chicken, sliced very thinly
2 tablespoons puréed or chopped garlic
1/2 cup French's canned fried onions
2 tablespoons vegetable oil

Dressing
1/2 teaspoon hot oil*
3 tablespoons soy sauce*
1 tablespoon sesame oil*
1 teaspoon lemon juice
1 teaspoon nam pla (fish sauce)*

Wash the asparagus and trim off the tough ends. Cut the asparagus on the diagonal into pieces about 1 inch long. Heat about 2 quarts of water to a boil and add the asparagus all at once. Leave in water about 1 minute then remove and chill in cold or iced water. When chilled, remove from water and place into paper towel lined salad bowl. Heat the oil in a wok or skillet until very hot but not smoking and sauté the garlic until it begins to turn golden then add chicken and cook chicken thoroughly. Remove the paper towel from asparagus. Add chicken and garlic to asparagus. Mix all the ingredients for dressing and toss with cooked chicken and asparagus. Sprinkle canned fried onions over top.

* These are Oriental ingredients available at many supermarkets and all Oriental markets.

Chicken Salad with Pineapple Dressing

Serves 4 to 6

1 1/2 pounds boneless, skinless chicken, cooked and diced
1/2 cup celery, diced
1/4 cup walnuts
1 cup seedless grapes sliced in half

Dressing Ingredients
1 cup mayonnaise
1/2 cup crushed pineapple
1 teaspoon Dijon mustard
salt and few dashes of Crystal hot sauce
salad greens

In a large bowl combine chicken, grapes, celery and walnuts. Combine mayonnaise, mustard and pineapple. Add hot sauce to taste, the sauce should be spicy. Toss with the other ingredients. Add salt to taste. Refrigerate. Serve on a bed of greens.

***Note**!* This is an all time favorite. In recent years it has become dangerous because it has been made with raw eggs. Here's a great recipe that does not include raw eggs and still has the taste and feel of a true Caesar Dressing.

Caesar Salad

Serves 4
1 small head romaine lettuce, about 1/2 pound
1/2 cup dressing,
approximately 1 cup croutons
1/4 cup Parmesan or Romano cheese (preferably shredded)

Wash lettuce and pat dry with paper towels. Cut across the rib into bite-size pieces. Place in salad bowl and toss with enough dressing to coat lettuce but not overwhelm it. Top with croutons and additional grated cheese if desired.

Caesar Salad Dressing

1 teaspoon garlic purée
1 teaspoon Worcestershire sauce
1 teaspoon anchovy paste
juice of 1/2 lemon
1 teaspoon Dijon mustard
1 cup mayonnaise, preferably with no sugar
1/2 cup grated Parmesan or Romano cheese
pinch paprika

Blend all ingredients in a food processor or mixer until well emulsified, about 2 minutes. The dressing will keep, well covered and refrigerated, for several weeks.

Three Vegetable Salad with Balsamic Vinaigrette

Serves 4 to 6
about 1 pound tomatoes
1 European cucumber
1 bell pepper
salt and pepper to taste
fresh basil and parsley, optional
shredded lettuce

Cut vegetables into dice. About 1 hour before serving toss with the dressing, and herbs. Shortly before serving season to taste. Serve on bed of shredded lettuce.

Balsamic Vinaigrette Dressing

1/4 cup balsamic vinegar
1 cup extra virgin olive oil
salt to taste

Mix ingredients thoroughly.

Cuban Black Bean and Rice Salad

Serves 4 to 6
1 can (15 or 16 ounce) black beans
2 cups cooked rice
1 cup finely chopped tomato
4 green onions, finely chopped
1/3 cup chilled fresh chopped coriander (cilantro)
1/2 cup extra virgin olive oil
2 tablespoons fresh lime juice or to taste
2 tablespoons Crystal hot sauce
salt and pepper to taste

Drain beans, rinse well and drain again. Combine beans with rice, tomato, onions and coriander and toss to mix. Combine olive oil, limejuice and hot sauce and whisk to mix and toss with salad ingredients. Salt and pepper to taste.

Caribbean Shrimp Salad

Serves 4
Mango Sauce (recipe follows)
2 cups cooked white rice
(use converted rice and follow directions on the box)
1 pound cooked, peeled, cold shrimp, preferably small ones
1 large, medium ripe, firm banana

Place mango sauce in bowl, peel banana and slice lengthwise into quarters and then slice crosswise to form small dice. Add banana to sauce and stir in rice. Stir in shrimp. If using large shrimp, cut in halves or thirds.

Mango Sauce

1 average size mango
1/4 cup Crystal hot sauce
juice of 2 medium limes
1/2 teaspoon salt or to taste

Peel, cut up, and purée mango. It should yield roughly 1 cup pulp. Add remaining ingredients and mix together thoroughly.

Tomato Salad with Feta

Serves 6
8 ounces Feta cheese, diced
2 pounds flavorful tomatoes, such as plum tomatoes
1 European cucumber
1/2 cup Calamata or Moroccan olives, pitted
extra virgin olive oil

Wash and coarsely chop the tomatoes and cucumber. Combine in salad dish and add the Feta cheese that has been diced. Toss in the whole olives and drizzle with olive oil. Allow to sit at room temperature about 15 minutes before serving.

Beef

No other animal or food stuff had as much influence on American history as did cattle. The Western push into The Territories (which became Texas, Oklahoma, Nebraska, etc.) was predominately for range land on which to graze herds of beef cattle. The torturously slow and massive cattle drives—and the cowboys who carried them out—moving the Texas longhorn to markets in Wichita and Abalene are the basic elements of American folklore. The romance of the open range was the fodder for books and later movies for a century and a half. The rail lines westward were built largely on the prospect of transport of cattle. Chicago was founded on the stockyards.

Beef was cheap and it fed the nation. Ours was the only country where even the poor could have beef and not just as a taste in a bowl of soup.

From the Texas Longhorn that yielded steaks as tough as shoe leather to the Shorthorn and improved Angus and Hereford that provide beef as tender and flavorful as any in the world, beef has been the backbone of the American cuisine.

A treasured memory of my teens was a Saturday when my daddy surprised me at my summer job by taking me out to lunch, just the two of us, at what could only be described as a dive, but which in our small town was famous for it's steaks. We each had a porterhouse about the size of a tennis racket, French fries, and iceberg lettuce salad. Because this was the south, there was brewed, sweet iced tea, glasses and glasses of it. Isn't it strange, after all these years, remembering the details of that lunch so well. It's probably true of all of us that many of our treasured memories are somehow involved with special foods or meals. I'm sure my daddy would have been pleased and surprised at how much such a spur of the moment event meant to me.

Pot Roast with Red Wine

Serves 8 with leftovers
6 to 8 pound beef roast, chuck or round are good choices
larding fat and twine—see note below
1/4 cup vegetable oil
1 bottle of red wine, 1 liter or fifth size
2 tablespoons garlic purée or 6 garlic cloves or granulated dry garlic
2 cups sliced onions
salt and pepper
1/3 cup flour
Preheat Oven to 325°F

*Ask butcher for beef fat sliced 1/8 to 1/4 inch thick in one piece, if possible, and a piece of butcher twine about 1 yard long, or buy a ball of kitchen twine.

   Place oil in a large, non-reactive pot (do not use aluminum) or roaster big and deep enough to hold roast. Over medium heat, brown the meat and onions thoroughly, turning frequently. When browned, remove the meat to cutting board and when cool enough to handle, cover the lean portions with fat and tie securely with string. Before returning meat to pan, **(see note) gradually stir in flour until onions are nicely coated and oil has been absorbed by flour. Cook over medium heat stirring very frequently. When mixture is a dark walnut brown, stir in wine, a bit at a time and stir each addition in well. Add garlic and return meat to pan. Cover pan, and place in oven and cook for 4 to 5 hours turning the meat every 30 minutes and stirring up gravy to prevent sticking. If gravy begins to look too thick, add 1/2 cup water and stir in thoroughly. The meat is ready when easily pierced by fork but holds together well enough to be sliced. Remove meat to platter, cut twine and remove fat. Cover with foil. Skim the fat off the gravy and add water if necessary to reach the gravy consistency you prefer. Taste for seasoning and add salt, pepper and garlic to taste.

** The gravy may be thickened after roasting. Just place meat in unthickened liquid and follow remainder of instructions. Make a roux by browning the 1/3 cup flour in 1/3 cup oil over medium heat, stirring frequently, because it burns easily, until a dark walnut brown. Set aside until roast is tender. Remove roast from pan and skim juices carefully. Place roasting pan on a burner over low heat, add roux, a bit at a time, and stir each addition until thoroughly blended. Correct gravy for seasoning.

To serve, slice beef and serve with gravy and potatoes, noodles or dumplings. Freeze leftovers in meal-size portions of sliced meat in gravy (allow a 4 to 6 ounce portion of meat and about 1/4 cup gravy per person).

Gourmet & Leftover Alert! *Of course, cooking a beef roast such as the one in the previous recipe takes a long time, and can't really be shortened, but the time for the average meal in that week can be short if you take advantage of recipes for leftovers such as the following one. Leftovers can make super meals*

Beef Pie

Serves 4
1 sheet frozen puff pastry dough
4 cups of diced pot roast and gravy
Preheat oven to 350°F

Thaw pastry thoroughly and unfold on large cutting board. Thaw meat, if necessary, and cut in 1/4 to 1/2 inch dice. Place cold meat and gravy in a gratin or pie dish. Lay pastry on top of dish and check that the pastry will cover the top of the container completely. If necessary, roll pastry to make a piece large enough to cover. Brush the lip of the container with water and lay pastry over. Press down to seal and with a sharp paring knife trim the pastry neatly around the sides. In the center of the pie cut a small (about 1/2 inch) hole to release steam. From the pastry scraps cut free-form petals and brush the area around the hole with water to stick down the petals to form a flower. To give a nice gloss to the pastry, brush lightly with milk or cream. Bake for about 45 minutes or until the pastry is a rich brown and the gravy and meat are hot.

Beef and Pasta Sauté

Serves 4 to 6
1 1/2 pounds lean beef round, thinly sliced
1 tablespoon vegetable oil
1 medium onion, peeled and sliced thinly, vertically
1 tablespoon minced garlic
1/2 bell pepper, thinly sliced
1 tablespoon chopped fresh basil
salt and black pepper to taste
1 can (1 pound) unseasoned crushed or diced tomatoes, or use fresh tomatoes (see directions below for skinning)
8 ounces penne or other small pieces of pasta
1 cup or more, if needed, water
1/2 cup grated Cheddar cheese

In a 2-quart pan sauté beef, onion, bell pepper and garlic in 1 tablespoon oil. Add tomato and basil and heat thoroughly then add pasta. Cover and simmer, stirring occasionally and adding water as needed, on low heat, for about 15 minutes or until pasta is cooked. Season to taste with salt and pepper. (Be enthusiastic with the pepper!) Sprinkle with cheese.

Note! *To skin tomatoes: Drop whole tomatoes into a pot of boiling water and remove in about 1 minute to a bowl of cold or ice water. As soon as they are cool enough to handle remove skins and use as desired.*

Gourmet Alert! *Many years ago, I read Mary Stewart's trilogy of novels about Merlin and the Arthurian Age. A pie similar to the one below was mentioned. My experiments produced the following result. This pie is so good you won't believe it. Everyone who eats oysters will love this pie. Since it uses readily available puff pastry dough for the piecrust it is simple as well as different and delicious.*

Beef and Oyster Pie

Serves 6
1 1/2 pounds lean beef round or chuck, cut in slivers
1 medium onion, peeled and thinly sliced vertically
1 tablespoon minced or puréed garlic
salt and pepper to taste
1/2 cup all-purpose flour
3 tablespoons vegetable oil
1/2 cup dry red wine broth or water
12 ounce container fresh oysters
1 frozen puff pastry dough sheet for crust, thawed
Preheat oven to 400°F

Make pastry topping (see directions to follow). Put flour in bowl or plastic bag add meat slices and toss lightly to cover. Heat oil in skillet and when hot add meat slices, without crowding, and brown. When brown, add onion and sauté until wilted and then add garlic, do not brown. Pour off visible oil and add wine and about 1/2 cup broth or water and simmer briefly to make a nice gravy. Salt and pepper to taste. Check oysters for bits of shell. If oysters are large cut into smaller pieces, add oysters and their liquid to the meat mixture and cook for about ten minutes. Remove to a gratin pan and top with the baked crust (below).

Pastry Topping

1 sheet frozen puff pastry

Remove 1 sheet from packet and store remaining sheet in freezer. Thaw pastry and when thawed, unfold and cut to fit within the opening of the gratin. Making the fit is easier if you place the gratin on the thawed dough and use the gratin as a guide for cutting the top. Carefully lift the cut pastry to a baking sheet. Brush top of pastry with cream and decorate with flowers or leaves cut from pastry scraps. Bake on foil lined cookie sheet and bake at 400°F or until puffed and well browned. Allow to cool before trying to remove from foil. Place on top of hot pie filling and run into 350°F oven for about ten minutes or until brown.

Cottage Pie

Serves 6
1 1/2 pounds lean beef round or chuck, cut in slivers
1/2 pound mushrooms, sliced coarsely
1 medium onion, peeled and thinly sliced from top to bottom
1 tablespoon minced or puréed garlic
salt and pepper to taste
1/2 cup all-purpose flour
3 tablespoons vegetable oil
1/2 cup dry red wine, broth or water
mashed potatoes (recipe follows)
Preheat oven to 350°F

Put flour in bowl or plastic bag add meat slices and toss lightly to cover. Heat oil in skillet and when hot add meat slices, without crowding, and brown. When brown, add mushrooms and onion and sauté until wilted then add garlic, do not brown. Pour off visible oil and add wine and about 1/2 cup broth or water and simmer briefly to make a nice gravy. Salt and pepper to taste. In same skillet, if it can go to table, or a 2 quart gratin pan, make a border around the edge with hillocks of mashed potato (see recipe below). Brown in oven for 15 to 20 minutes or until potato topping is an attractive brown.

<u>Note</u>! *This mashed potato recipe is not as rich as the one in the Vegetable section. This one has less butter. The pie is so rich that I thought it best that the potatoes not be.*

Mashed Potatoes

>2 pounds, approximately, white potatoes (Red Bliss are nice and if skins are thin, as on new potatoes, they need not be peeled)
>2 tablespoons butter
>about 1/2 cup whole milk
>salt to taste

Cut potatoes in quarters, to peel or not to peel that's up to you, place in a sauce pan and cover with cold water, add about 1 teaspoon salt. Boil for about 20 minutes or until tender. Pour off water and put pan back on heat to dry water from pan. Add milk to pan to warm and mash potatoes with masher. If skin was left on it will not be possible to get potatoes really smooth. Add butter and stir or mash until melted. Season to taste and use on pie.

Beef Stroganoff

Serves 4 to 6

1 1/2 pounds steak, round or sirloin, thinly sliced
6 tablespoons butter
3/4 cup peeled, slivered onion, sliced from top to bottom of onion
12 ounces mushrooms, trimmed at cap and sliced
1 teaspoon Dijon mustard
1 tablespoon minced garlic
3 heaping tablespoons flour
1/2 cup broth, beef or chicken
1/2 cup, or as needed, half & half
1/2 cup or more, sour cream
salt and pepper to taste

Melt 4 tablespoons of the butter in a large, heavy skillet and when it is sizzling, add mushrooms and sauté, stirring frequently, until they are very nicely browned, about 20 minutes. Remove mushrooms from skillet and add meat, stirring until seared, remove from skillet with a slotted spoon, leaving butter and juices behind. Add meat and remaining butter to skillet, stirring until seared. Remove from skillet and add to mushrooms. Add onion to skillet and sauté until well wilted and then add flour, stirring in well and cook for about 2 minutes. Add mustard and garlic and stir to blend. Add broth and half & half and stir and cook until sauce is desired consistency then return meat and mushrooms to pan and heat thoroughly. If sauce looks too thick, add more broth and/or half & half. Season to taste with salt and black pepper. Stir in sour cream and heat thoroughly but do not boil. Serve over noodles or with mashed potatoes.

Gourmet Alert! *This is a perennial favorite. This recipe for Sauerbraten is about as simple as it can get, and still it's rather elaborate, and takes advance planning. Well they can't all be made easy. Try it!*

Sauerbraten and Dumplings

Serves 6 to 8 with leftovers
4 to 5 pound lean pot roast
2 tablespoons oil
1 medium onion, chopped
2 carrots chopped
1/2 cup water
1/2 to 1 cup gingersnap crumbs
marinade (includes the following)
1/2 cup wine vinegar
1 1/2 cups red wine
1/2 cup water
1/2 teaspoon black pepper or 10 peppercorns (remove before making gravy)
1 teaspoon ground cinnamon
3 bay leaves
1 medium onion, chopped

Rinse roast and place, together with chopped onion in a glass or plastic container to marinate. Combine marinade ingredients, except onion and bring to light boil, remove from heat, add reserved onion and pour marinade over roast. Cover and refrigerate. Turn roast twice daily for 2 to 3 days. About 4 hours before serving, remove roast from marinade and dry with paper towels. Heat the oil in a heavy, non-reactive (non-aluminum) oven safe pan with a lid. Brown the roast thoroughly. When well browned, pour in marinade, water, onion and carrot. Cover and cook at 325°F until tender but not falling apart (about 3 hours). Remove roast from pan and make gravy. Remove bay leaves and peppercorns from pan. Remove vegetables and purée them and return to pan. Thicken with gingersnap crumbs, adding a small amount at a time until thickened to desired thickness. Season to taste. Serve with Dumplings below.

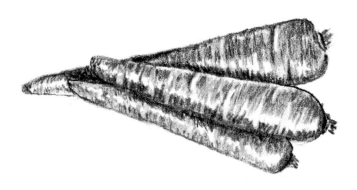

Dumplings

2 cups self-rising flour
1 large egg, beaten
3 tablespoons oil
2/3 cup milk or enough liquid to make a stiff dough

Bring about 4 quarts of water with 2 teaspoons salt to a boil in a pan with a lid. Combine egg, oil and 1/2 liquid and beat. Stir this mixture into flour and mix, adding additional liquid as needed, until dough is just stiff. Drop dough in tablespoon-size balls into the boiling water. Reduce heat to simmer and cover pan. Cover and cook for about 12 minutes until dumplings float. Remove from water and serve.

Beef Bolognese

Serves 4 to 6

6 beef top round steaks, about 4 ounces each
(have your butcher tenderize them once)
grated Parmesan cheese
flour, about 1/2 cup
2 tablespoons vegetable oil
2 tablespoons butter
1 heaping teaspoon chopped garlic
1 medium onion, diced
1/2 cup, approximately, red wine
2 tablespoons heavy cream or sour cream
salt and pepper

Salt and pepper meat liberally and dust lightly with flour. Heat oil and butter together in a skillet until it is sizzling but not browning. Brown the meat on both sides, without crowding, in skillet, if necessary, cook in two batches, adding more oil and butter if needed. When meat is browned place a tablespoon of Parmesan on each piece and cover the skillet with a lid and cook over low heat for about 10 minutes. Remove meat and keep warm. Deglaze the pan with the wine and add the cream. Season to taste and pour sauce over meat.

<u>**Note!**</u> *Deglazing is adding liquid to a pan that has been used for sautéing, in order to soften the juices and crispy bits clinging to the pan, thus making the foundation for a sauce.*

Timesaver Alert! Well we just hit the deep south again! Grillades, grits, and New Orleans roast beef Po Boys are staples in New Orleans and Cajun country. Once you try them you'll see why. Grillades are traditionally made with veal. Here they're made with beef.

Grillades and Grits

Serves 4

1 1/4 pounds round steak cut about 1/4 inch thick
1 large onion
1 heaping teaspoon chopped garlic
1/2 bell pepper (optional)
few sprigs of parsley, chopped
3 tablespoons butter
8 ounces mushrooms, sliced
1 large or 2 medium, tomatoes, diced
1/2 cup dry red wine
1 cup flour
1 teaspoon each salt and pepper
Quick grits

Cut steak in 4 portions and spread flour on a piece of waxed paper and stir in salt and pepper, distributing evenly. Place rinsed and wet steak on the seasoned flour and turn until both sides are well coated with flour. Melt butter in skillet and when it is sizzling add the steak portions. Don't allow them to touch or they will steam instead of browning. Brown lightly on both sides and remove from pan and set aside. Add vegetables to pan and cook until softened. Add wine and stir contents to mix. Return steak to pan, cover and reduce heat to low and cook for about 30 minutes. Taste gravy for seasoning and add salt and pepper as needed. Serve with quick grits for 4, prepared according to package directions.

New Orleans Roast Beef

Serves 6 to 8 with lots of leftovers
choose a lean, boneless roast, about 4 pounds
salt, pepper and garlic
Preheat oven to 300°F

Rinse roast and salt and pepper liberally. In a few tablespoons of vegetable oil, brown the roast deeply until it is a rich chestnut brown. Place roast in roaster pan with lid and deglaze browning pan with water or red wine. There should be an inch or so of liquid in the roaster at all times. Put a heaping tablespoon of chopped garlic (or to taste) in liquid. Roast, turning occasionally, for 3 to 4 hours or until fork tender. The pan drippings are a delicious gravy. This roast with gravy is wonderful over mashed potatoes, See Vegetable Chapter.

Leftover Alert! *Once you've got the roast, you have to try this Po Boy sandwich. It is possibly the best you'll ever find. In addition there are several other recipes which follow, that are handy to use up leftover roast.*

Roast Beef Po Boy

Serves 4 to 6
1 French baguette split lengthwise
tomato slices to cover
shredded lettuce to cover
mayonnaise
sliced hot roast beef
hot gravy

Spread one side of baguette with mayonnaise. On other side put layers of beef, tomato and lettuce then gravy over all. Cut baguette into 4 to 6 pieces. Serve Immediately.

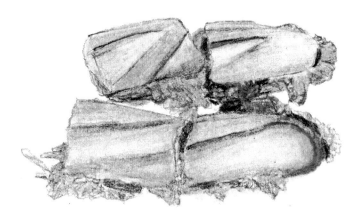

Pasta with Roast Beef Sauce

Serves 4
12 ounces pasta, cooked and hot
2 cups chopped hot beef with gravy

Combine and serve.

Roast Beef Hash

Serves 6
1 medium onion, chopped finely or 5 green onions, sliced
3 tablespoons butter and 2 tablespoons vegetable oil
1 1/2 to 2 cups white potato, diced finely (if using Red Bliss, it may not be necessary to peel)
2 1/2 cups roast beef, diced
1/2 cup beef gravy or heavy cream
salt and pepper to taste

Put butter and oil in a 9 or 10-inch skillet and heat until it sizzles. Add potato and cook turning frequently until browned on all sides. Add onion and sauté until it is soft but not brown. Add beef and cook for about 3 to 4 minutes. Stir gravy or cream into mixture, and stir and mash in until the whole mass is lightly browned. Season to taste.

Hash Gratin

Serves 6
2 tablespoons butter
1 large onion, diced finely
2 1/2 cups roast beef, diced finely
salt, pepper and Worcestershire sauce to taste
1 cup beef gravy
3 cups seasoned mashed potatoes
Preheat oven to 350°F

Sauté onion in the butter until soft then add beef and sauté to heat and mix well. Add gravy, heat and then season. Separately, make a layer of the mashed potatoes in a gratin pan which has been well sprayed with pan spray. Pour beef mix over. Bake for about 25 minutes or until browned but not dry.

Steak Sandwiches Sublime

Serves 1
1 small beef filet (tenderloin) steak (about 4 ounces)
1 tablespoon soft butter per sandwich
1/2 cup sliced mushrooms per sandwich
1 green onion, finely chopped, per sandwich
grainy mustard
crisp lettuce
individual size French bread loaf, warmed

In a small skillet heat butter until it sizzles and sauté steak at moderately high heat until at desired doneness, do not overcook; filet is lean and becomes tough when overcooked. Remove from pan and keep warm while sautéing mushrooms and onion. When done set aside. Slice the French bread lengthwise, and spread with grainy mustard then put the steak on the bottom slice of bread and top with the mushrooms, onion and pan dripping and salt to taste. Lastly, add the lettuce leaf. Enjoy!

Gourmet & Timesaver Alert! *For a special breakfast or brunch, you will want to try this recipe. It is simple, quick and so delicious and elegant you won't believe it.*

Creamed Chipped Beef in Vol au Vent Shells

Serves 6 for breakfast or light supper
1 package frozen patty shells baked according to package directions
3 tablespoons butter or more as needed
3 tablespoons flour
6 medium mushrooms, about 1/3 pound, finely diced
1 medium shallot or 4 green onions, finely diced
1 small jar dried beef cut into pieces
1 cup milk or as needed
salt and black pepper to taste
Dash of Tabasco to taste

Melt butter in medium skillet and when it sizzles add shallot or green onion and mushrooms. Sauté until wilted, adding more butter if needed and then add beef and cook until it begins to frizzle. Add more butter if needed and stir in flour. Cook and stir for about 3 minutes then stir in milk until it is of desired consistency. Serve in hot patty shells. (It may be served over biscuits, toast, mashed potatoes or grits if preferred). Note: 1/2 cup of grated sharp Cheddar cheese may be stirred in at the last minute.

Gourmet Alert! *In Europe one of the most popular sauces for steaks pavé (thick nearly cubical cuts of meat shaped like paving stones or cobbles) is Poivre Vert which means green peppercorn. This approximation of that sauce is quick but grand.*

Sautéed Filets Poivre Vert

Serves 2

2 tablespoons butter approximately 4 to 6 ounces of filet per person
1 rounded teaspoon crushed brine packed green peppercorns, drained (see note below)
1 teaspoon finely chopped garlic
2 tablespoons flour
1/2 cup, approximately, dry red wine
1/4 cup heavy cream
salt and black pepper to taste

In a skillet just large enough to hold filets without touching, heat butter until it sizzles. Rinse and dry filets and sauté in the hot butter. Brown on each side but keep rare. When desired state of doneness is reached, remove filets from pan. Add crushed peppercorns and garlic to pan and sauté briefly. Add flour to peppercorns and garlic and cook, stirring, for 2 to 3 minutes. Stir in wine until well blended then add cream, stirring to blend. Season to taste with salt and pepper then spoon over steaks.

Note! Peppercorns are readily available in cans at Oriental markets. Repacked in their liquid, in a jar with a secure lid, they will keep for months in the refrigerator.

Garlic and Ginger Beef with Coconut Rice

Serves 4

1 pound tender beef such as sirloin or tenderloin
1 teaspoon grated or chopped fresh ginger
1 teaspoon grated or chopped garlic
2 tablespoons soy sauce (regular not "Lite")
1/4 teaspoon crushed red pepper
1 bunch green onions
2 tablespoons vegetable oil

Slice the beef into thin strips, removing all tough bits and fat chunks. Combine ginger, garlic, soy and pepper and press into surface of the beef. Clean the green onions and cut into pieces about 1 inch long and set aside. Heat the oil in a wok or skillet until very hot but not smoking and add the beef all at once. Cook, stirring, for about a minute and add onion. Cook until onion is wilted and beef cooked. Serve atop the coconut rice, recipe follows.

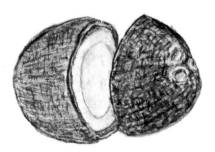

<u>Note!</u> *Grated ginger (ginger purée) can be found, refrigerated, at some supermarkets. If using fresh ginger (pieces of ginger are called "hands") buy hands that are plump and solid. Grate the amount you need and store the remainder, wrapped in a plastic bag or in a closed jar, in the freezer.*

Coconut Rice

1 cup converted rice
1 can (13.5 ounce) unsweetened coconut milk
1/4 cup (2 ounces) water
1/4 teaspoon salt or to taste
2 tablespoons butter

In a heavy pot with lid, melt the butter and when it sizzles, add the rice and cook, stirring occasionally until the rice grains begin to turn golden. Stir in the coconut milk and salt and use the water to swirl around the can to loosen the remaining coconut residue, then add to the rice. Be sure to break up all lumps. Cook on low heat, tightly covered, for about 25 minutes, stirring occasionally to prevent sticking. Alternatively, bake, tightly covered in a 350°F oven for about 35 minutes, stirring occasionally. This rice will be rather sticky because of the coconut.

Beef with Mushrooms

Serves 4 to 6

1 pound beef (top round or sirloin), sliced very thinly
1 cup sliced mushrooms
2 teaspoons puréed garlic
1 medium onion
3 tablespoons flour
1/2 cup red wine
1/2 cup sour cream or as needed
3 tablespoons vegetable oil
12 ounces pasta, cooked and hot

Slice the beef into thin strips, removing all tough bits and fat chunks. Combine beef with garlic and flour and press into the surface of the beef. Peel the onion and cut it into half from top to bottom. Slice each half into thin semicircles. Wash the mushrooms and slice thinly. Heat the oil in a wok or skillet until very hot, but not smoking, and add the beef all at once. Cook, stirring, and separating pieces until the slices begin to brown, then add onion and mushrooms. Cook until onion and mushrooms are wilted and beef cooked. Add the wine and bring to a boil then turn down heat and simmer and reduce for 2 or 3 minutes. Stir in the sour cream. Simmer and stir the mixture until a nice sauce forms. If it looks too thick then add a bit more sour cream. Season to taste with salt and pepper. Serve over pasta.

Sesame Beef

Serves 4
1 pound beef (round or sirloin), sliced very thinly
2 tablespoons puréed or chopped garlic
2 tablespoons soy sauce (use regular not "Lite")
3 tablespoons Oriental sesame oil*
1/2 teaspoon hot oil*
1 medium onion
2 tablespoons vegetable oil

Slice the beef thinly, removing all tough bits and fat chunks. Combine sesame oil, garlic, soy sauce and pepper and press into the surface of the beef. Peel the onion and cut it into half from top to bottom. Slice each half into thin semicircles. Heat the oil in a wok or skillet until very hot but not smoking and add the beef all at once. Cook, stirring, for about a minute and add onion. Cook until onion is wilted and beef cooked. Serve with plain rice.

Beef Curry

Serves 4
1 pound beef, sliced very thinly
2 tablespoons chopped garlic
1 tablespoon Thai red curry paste*
1 medium onion
1/2 cup unsweetened coconut milk
1 teaspoon lemon juice
1 teaspoon fish sauce (nam pla)*
2 tablespoons vegetable oil

Slice the beef thinly, removing all tough bits and fat chunks. Peel the onion and cut it into half from top to bottom. Slice each half into thin semicircles. Heat the oil in a wok or skillet until very hot but not smoking and add the beef and cook briefly until it begins to color. Then add the curry paste and the garlic and cook, stirring, for about a minute; add onion. Cook until onion is wilted and beef cooked. Add the coconut milk, lemon juice and fish sauce. Cook, stirring until sauce is formed. Salt to taste. Serve with plain rice.

* Oriental items available at many supermarkets, and all Oriental markets

Timesaver Alert! *What a wonderful recipe this is! The beef is sliced thinly, and therefore the cooking time is short. But when you eat it you won't believe it took so little time.*

Beef with Saga Blue and Potatoes

Serves 4 to 6
1 pound beef (top round or sirloin), sliced very thinly
1 tablespoon puréed or chopped garlic
6 ounces Saga blue cheese
2 tablespoons butter
1/4 cup sour cream
1 1/2 pounds Red Bliss potatoes
salt and pepper to taste

If potato skins are tender, do not peel potatoes, just dice them (1/2 inch pieces). Place potatoes into sauce pan large enough to hold them easily. Cover potatoes with cold water and add 1 teaspoon salt. Bring potatoes to boil and reduce heat to a simmer. If potatoes reach firm-tender before beef is done, turn heat off and keep potatoes hot. Slice the beef thinly, removing all tough bits and fat chunks and toss with garlic. Melt butter in separate skillet and when it is sizzling but not turning brown add the beef and sauté until no red shows. Reduce heat and stir in cheese. Stir until cheese melts and stir in sour cream. Season to taste with salt and pepper. Drain potatoes and add to skillet and toss to cover with sauce.

Leftover Alert! *Here's another great way to use leftovers.*

Country Beef Pie

Serves 4 to 6
4 cups trimmed and diced leftover roast beef
1 medium to large onion, peeled quartered and thinly sliced
2 cups sliced mushrooms
2 tablespoons butter
2 cup gravy
biscuits, recipe follows
salt and pepper to taste
Preheat oven to 375°F

Melt butter in a skillet at high heat until it sizzles and sauté onion and mushrooms, stirring frequently, until they begin to brown. In separate pan, combine beef and gravy and heat until it is almost boiling. Place in baking dish large enough to contain about 2 quarts. Add sautéed mushroom and onion and stir into the gravy then top with the biscuit rounds. Bake until biscuits are browned and completely cooked, about 15 to 20 minutes. Check on doneness by lifting a biscuit to see if bottom looks cooked and isn't wet and "doughy".

Buttermilk Biscuits

12 to 14 biscuits (about 2 inch diameter)
2 cups self-rising flour
1/4 cup solid vegetable shortening
1 cup (more or less) buttermilk

Cut shortening into flour with a table fork until the dough resembles cookie crumbs. Stir in buttermilk (the secret of good biscuits) about 1/3 at a time until the dough is well moistened but not soppy wet. Turn out onto lightly floured piece of wax paper and pat and knead gently into a ball and then flatten to about 1/4 to 1/2 inch thick (thinner biscuits are crisper and thicker have a softer crumb). Cut into rounds with 1-inch cutter and place on pie filling.

Bookmaker Sandwich

Per person
2 slices of sourdough bread
4 ounces, approximately, sliced beef filet
butter
1 to 2 ounces crumbled Roquefort or Stilton cheese
1 tablespoons beef or bacon dripping or butter
Leaf of lettuce

Butter both slices of bread and crumble the cheese over one. Heat the skillet very hot and melt the dripping or butter and sauté the meat about 2 minutes per side or until medium rare. Place the steak on the cheese, add lettuce and top with the buttered bread slice. Slice sandwich and eat at once.

Filet BLT

Serves 1

2 slices of sourdough bread
3 ounces, approximately, sliced beef filet
3 strips bacon
2 medium slices ripe tomato
leaf of romaine or leaf lettuce
mayonnaise
2 tablespoons bacon dripping or butter

Spread both slices of bread with mayonnaise and place the tomato on one slice. Fry the bacon until crisp and place on paper towels to drain. Heat the skillet very hot and melt the dripping or butter and sauté the meat about 2 minutes per side or until medium rare. Place the steak on the tomato then place the bacon on the filet then add the lettuce and the second slice of bread. Slice and eat immediately.

Pork

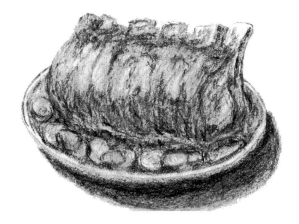

Southerners have always been partial to pork. In early times this was because pork could rather easily be smoked and so would keep indefinitely without refrigeration. Pigs are easier to raise than cows, less vulnerable to insects and extremes of climate and in hard times they were able to survive by foraging for their food in the forest. There used to be a saying in the south that if a lady had a good black dress and a country ham she could face any social situation. Readers will notice that I use country ham in many ways, as seasoning or on its own. When one thinks of traditional southern food, ham, biscuits, and fried chicken come to mind. They are great on their own, but taken together they are nectar of the Gods.

Pork is a mild flavored meat and takes readily to sauces. Pork can be used interchangeably with veal and chicken in most instances. Almost every part of the pig can be utilized, giving rise to the saying that you can use "Everything but the squeal."

Gourmet Alert! *Bourbon is one of the great whiskeys of the world. Evan Williams is credited with being the first operator of a distillery in Kentucky, in Bourbon County. The whiskey took its name from there. Bourbon was made from the native American grain, corn. The subtle sweetness of Bourbon has made it a natural partner with other favorite southern foods, such as pecans and ham.*

Baked Ham with Bourbon and Brown Sugar Glaze

whole or portion of fully cooked, lightly cured ham
Glaze Includes
2 cups brown sugar
1/4 cup Dijon mustard
1 ounce Bourbon whiskey
Preheat oven to 350°F

Mix the ingredients for the glaze. Remove skin and pat glaze on the fat side of the fully cooked ham. The glaze should be thick in order to keep the glaze from running off. Bake ham uncovered until glaze begins to caramelize and moisture begins to form in the pan. Any leftover glaze can be refrigerated for later use.

Note! *Fully cooked ham: If you are using other than Country Ham, you may find the flavor of the ham mild to non-existent. The fully cooked ham has the virtue of being quicker to prepare. The cooking you do to it at home should be directed toward improving flavor and reducing the excessive moisture. Figure about 1/2 pound of ham for each person served. Of course, you will want to buy enough so that there are plenty leftovers. If you are buying half of a ham, the butt half (the wide end) will yield more attractive slices and usable meat. Save the bone to make broth for soup or to cook with beans or greens.*

Timesaver & Leftover Alert! *Did you have some ham leftover from the baked ham you fixed for guests? Well, the next recipe is for you. It's a great way to serve leftovers that makes them seem totally new. Go out and buy some cooked ham if you have to, this recipe is great! Almost all the time taken is when the gratin is in the oven and you are free for other things.*

Note! *In the next recipe use the following timesaving trick.*

Beating Eggs: When I am beating egg whites and yolks separately, as is often the case, I always beat the whites first, while the beaters are clean. Whites will not beat if any yellow is present. On the other hand the yellows and the batter they are usually in don't care if there are egg whites present. So, beat the whites first, and there is no need to wash the beaters until the recipe is done.

Ham and Cheese Gratin

Serves 4
2 cups finely chopped ham
1 1/2 cups grated cheese, Cheddar, Swiss or Gruyére
4 large eggs, separated
4 tablespoons soft butter
1 heaping tablespoon Dijon or grainy mustard
dash hot sauce
Preheat oven to 350°F

Beat egg whites until they hold stiff peaks. Set them aside. In another large bowl, cream the butter, add egg yolks and beat until fluffy (no need to wash beaters before this step). Add ham, cheese, mustard and hot sauce to butter mixture and fold in thoroughly by hand. Fold in egg whites gently, again by hand. Don't taste sauce after raw eggs have been added until it has been fully cooked. Pour the mixture into a well greased 2 quart casserole, about 1 1/2 inches deep, bake until puffed in center and lightly browned, about 30 minutes.

Sautéed Pork Chops

Serves 4 to 6

4 to 6 thick cut boneless chops
1 cup all-purpose flour
2 tablespoons butter
2 tablespoons vegetable oil
1/2 cup dry white wine
salt and black pepper
1 tablespoon Dijon mustard
1 teaspoon minced garlic
1/2 cup cream or half & half
few sprigs parsley, chopped

Pour flour onto a piece of wax paper about 18 inches long. Add the salt and pepper (about 1 teaspoon of each) to flour and coat pork chops. Allow them to dry for about 5 minutes. Choose a skillet large enough to hold chops without crowding (else they will steam). Add oil and swirl around bottom of pan so bottom is coated. Add butter, and when it is sizzling hot, add chops and cover, leaving cover slightly askew to allow some of the steam to escape. Turn about every 5 minutes so they will brown well and evenly. Cook for about 20 minutes or until still lightly pink in center. Remove from pan and set aside while making sauce. Pour off all but about 1 tablespoon of fat from pan and add mustard, garlic and wine. Stir and deglaze pan. Taste for seasoning and add salt and pepper if desired. Add cream and stir to reduce slightly. Pour sauce over chops to serve. Noodles are a good companion.

Timesaver & Leftover Alert! *The next two recipes show ways to use baked ham leftovers. Be sure to trim off all the remaining glaze, which would add too much sweetness to this sandwich.*

Ham and Cheese Rolls

Serves 4
1 package refrigerated crescent roll dough
4 ounces thinly sliced cooked country ham or if using deli ham, choose a type which isn't sweet.
4 to 5 ounces grated Monterey Jack or Cheddar cheese
8 ounces sliced fresh mushrooms (optional)
1 ounce butter
Preheat oven to 350°F

If using mushrooms, sauté them in the butter and allow them to cool. Unroll dough, taking care not to stretch it. Divide along perforations. Divide ham, cheese and mushrooms among rolls and roll up, starting from wide end of the triangle. Carefully transfer rolls to baking sheet lined with foil that has been sprayed with pan spray. Bake for about 20 minutes or until puffed and golden. These are great with scrambled eggs for brunch.

Ham and Egg Cobbler

Serves 4

Sauce

4 tablespoons butter
4 tablespoons flour
2 cups milk, approximately
1/2 teaspoon mustard powder
salt and pepper to taste

In a saucepan or skillet, at least 1 quart size, melt the butter over medium heat and stir in flour. Cook and stir for about two minutes and then stir milk in gradually. Allow sauce to thicken then salt and pepper to taste and whisk in mustard.

Filling

1/2 pound cooked ham, cut into julienne or dice
4 hard-boiled large eggs, peeled and quartered lengthwise
4 green onions, sliced in thin rounds

Grease or spray with pan spray a shallow baking dish about 10 inches in diameter. Spread the filling evenly and pour sauce over. Top with cobbles, below.

Cobbles

2 cups self-rising flour
1/3 cup soft shortening or butter
1 cup buttermilk, approximately
1 cup grated sharp Cheddar cheese
Preheat oven to 375°F

Stir shortening into flour and moisten well with buttermilk, the mixture should be wet but not sloppy then stir in cheese. With two tablespoons make balls about 1 inch diameter. Place over filling in pan. Bake for about 25 to 30 minutes or until the cobbles are nicely browned and the filling bubbly.

Pork Schnitzel

Serves 6

1 1/2 pounds thin, boneless, pork loin chops, flattened or ask your butcher to tenderize them
2 or 3 slices of fresh white bread made into crumbs
1/2 cup all-purpose flour
2 large eggs, beaten
3 tablespoons butter
2 tablespoons oil
salt and pepper to taste

Rinse chops, dip into beaten egg. Salt and pepper them, lightly, and then dip both sides into the crumb-flour mixture that has been spread on a sheet of wax paper. Be sure they are thoroughly covered. Place on waxed paper and allow to dry for about 20 minutes. Heat the oil and butter in a skillet large enough to hold the cutlets without crowding or cook them in two batches, keeping the first batch warm in a low oven while the second cooks. Sauté about 3 minutes per side or until golden brown and done. Pour off oil and deglaze pan with cream or half & half. Season to taste. Serve with Spaetzele. See recipe below.

Note! *Deglazing is adding liquid to a pan which has been used for sautéing, in order to soften the juices and crispy bits clinging to the pan, thus making the foundation for a sauce.*

Spaetzele

2 large eggs
2 tablespoons vegetable oil or melted butter
1/2 cup water
1/2 cup milk
2 1/2 cups all-purpose flour
1/2 teaspoon salt
1/2 teaspoon baking powder

Fill a large pot with water, 3 or 4 quarts, and add about 2 teaspoons salt to water. Bring to a boil.

Mix all liquids, including eggs, and blend well. Combine dry ingredients and combine with liquids. The resulting dough will be quite stiff.

The spaetzele can be cooked by dropping dough by spoonfuls into the boiling water but this will be VERY slow. A spaetzele maker can be made as follows:

Use a coffee can with holes cut in the bottom to hold the raw dough and to press out "strings" of spaetzele into the boiling water. The holes can be conveniently made in the bottom of the coffee can with a "church key" (one of those old beer can openers that has a triangular knife-like device at the end that you use to puncture tinned milk and other cans of liquid. The dough can be pushed through the holes in the bottom of the can with a soft spatula or a potato masher that has been covered with foil. Spaetzele will float when done. Cooking takes about 5 minutes.

Leftover Alert! *The next two recipes are good ways to use leftovers.*

Sweet Potato and Ham Medley

Serves 4

1 1/2 to 2 cups peeled and diced sweet potatoes
2 1/2 cups diced ham
5 green onions, sliced
2 tablespoons vegetable (not olive) oil
3 tablespoons butter
1/2 cup heavy cream
2 tablespoons butter
salt and pepper to taste

Parboil the potato dice for 3 minutes and drain. Heat the butter and oil until it sizzles and sauté the potato until it begins to brown then add onion and cook until it begins to wilt. Add the ham and cook for about 5 minutes then add cream and stir in until most is absorbed. Season to taste.

Note! *Sweet Potatoes: Wear kitchen gloves to peel and dice sweet potatoes because they will turn your hands yellow!*

Ham and Asparagus Bread Pudding

Serves 4

about 8 ounces home-style white bread, dry or toasted
1/2 pound cooked ham, diced or julienne
3/4 pound, approximately, blanched fresh asparagus, reserve about 4 spears
1/4 pound Gruyére or Swiss cheese, grated
1/4 pound sharp Cheddar cheese, grated
1/2 cup shredded Parmesan, reserve 2 tablespoons for top
1/2 cup chopped green onion or parsley
3 cups milk, warmed
4 large eggs, beaten
1 teaspoon each salt and black pepper
Preheat oven to 350°F

Grease or spray a shallow 2 quart baking dish with pan spray. Whip together the eggs, milk and salt and pepper. In bottom of baking dish, make a layer of bread and top with 1/3 the grated cheeses and 1/2 the ham and asparagus. Make another layer of bread, cheeses, ham and asparagus. Top with remaining bread and cheese and pour liquid mix over all. Allow the liquid time to thoroughly soak the bread, occasionally pressing down gently. Sprinkle the Parmesan over and bake at 350°F approximately 1 hour or until the interior is at 170°F and top is a rich golden. Before serving, top with the reserved asparagus spears. Serve hot.

Gourmet & Timesaver Alert! *Everyone will love this, especially the cook. It's a breeze to do but it tastes wonderful. It's truly an example of the fact that gourmet cooking need not take much time, just thought.*

Oriental Pork Burgers

Serves 4

1 1/4 pounds, approximately, ground pork
1 shallot or small onion, finely diced
2 teaspoons garlic, finely diced
2 tablespoons regular soy sauce
1/2 teaspoon ginger, grated or finely chopped
3 or 4 dashes of hot sauce such as Crystal
1/4 cup mushrooms, finely diced
package of Kaiser rolls or hamburger buns
Oriental Pork Burger Sauce, below

Mix all ingredients thoroughly and form into patties about 1/2 inch thick. In a skillet large enough to hold patties without crowding, heat 2 tablespoons of vegetable oil and sauté the patties until juices run clear and internal temperature is 170°F. Remove from heat and place on buns and top with the following sauce.

Oriental Pork Burger Sauce

1 cup mayonnaise
1 small tomato, finely chopped
1 heaping teaspoon Dijon mustard
1 green onion, finely chopped
2 teaspoons capers

Combine all ingredients and refrigerate until needed. Heap a tablespoonful or as desired on each patty after placing on bottom half of bun but before putting on the top.

Gourmet Alert! *This is a wonderful and unusual recipe. Don't let the garlic deter you. No flavor is overwhelming.*

Roast Pork Mistral

Serves 4 to 6
3 pound loin of pork
1/3 cup flour
1 teaspoon salt
1 teaspoon black pepper
3 tablespoons vegetable oil
2 bulbs garlic
fresh rosemary sprigs
1/2 cup or to taste, dry, red wine
Preheat oven to 350°F

Combine flour, salt and pepper on a sheet of wax paper. Rinse the roast and while still damp, place roast on the floured paper and give it a thorough coating on all sides. Let rest for about five minutes and if any part of the roast looks damp, re-flour it. Reserve remainder of flour. Break the garlic bulbs into cloves but do not peel. Fill a small saucepan about half full of water and bring to a boil. Boil the garlic cloves about 1 minute and then drain. As soon as they are cool enough to handle, peel them. Heat the oil and brown the roast on all sides in a heavy oven-proof pan, with a lid. (The pan should be just large enough to hold the roast.) When the roast is brown, insert the tip of a sharp knife in five or six places on top of roast and insert a small sprig of rosemary in each hole. Lift roast and place peeled garlic cloves under it. Cover the roaster and place in oven. Roast for about 1 1/2 hours or until internal temperature is 160°F. Remove roast and garlic from pan and set aside, keeping warm while making gravy. Pour off all but about 3 tablespoons of dripping and add about 3 tablespoons of the reserved flour. Stir in enough flour so there is no visible oil. Stir and cook flour over low heat until nicely browned. Gently stir in wine and enough broth or water to make gravy of desired consistency. Season to taste. Slice roast and serve with garlic cloves surrounding. Serve with potatoes or dumplings.

Timesaver Alert! *There is nothing that says "Southern Cookin'" as emphatically as Country fried steak. The next recipe is a take-off on that theme using pork. It's quick and easy to fix, and just wonderful fun.*

Pork Country Fried Steak

Serves 4

1 1/2 to 2 cutlets per person (4 to 6 ounces per person)
all-purpose flour
salt, pepper
3 tablespoons vegetable oil
1 teaspoon garlic, chopped or puréed
milk, about 1 cup
butter as needed (see gravy below)
3 tablespoons flour

Purchase thinly sliced, boneless pork chops, and have the butcher tenderize them TWICE. Rinse cutlets. Combine about 1/2 cup flour and about 1/2 teaspoon each, salt and black pepper and spread on a sheet of wax paper. Flour the cutlets thoroughly, mashing lightly to make a good coating. Heat the oil until sizzling (very hot but not smoking) in a skillet large enough to hold chops without crowding. (If necessary cook in two batches.) Sauté the cutlets until well browned, but do not overcook. If necessary add more oil to pan. Keep warm in oven while making gravy.

Country Gravy

To make gravy, add butter if needed to oil in skillet to bring total to 3 tablespoons. Use flour from that used to cover the cutlets and additional flour if necessary to make a total of 3 tablespoons of flour. Stir flour into the hot oil in skillet, and cook for about 2 minutes, stirring any crunchy bits in pan. Stir in enough milk to make a smooth gravy about the consistency of heavy cream. Stir in finely chopped garlic. Taste for seasonings, adding salt and pepper if necessary. Serve with mashed potatoes, white rice, or biscuits.

Gourmet Alert! *This is a delightful recipe I evolved from the traditional Cordon Bleu using pork rather than veal, and doing things in a less than traditional way with no loss in flavor or fun. Cordon Bleu was popular in this country in the 1950's and has gone out of style. Too bad. It's great!*

Pork Cutlets "Cordon Bleu"

Serves 1, multiply as needed
1 1/2 to 2 cutlets (4 ounces each) per person
Proscuitto to cover each cutlet, about 1/2 of a thin slice
1 slice Gruyére cheese per cutlet
flour
butter
half & half or cream

Purchase thinly sliced, boneless pork chops and have the butcher tenderize them TWICE. Use just enough butter to film the bottom of the skillet when butter is melted. Rinse cutlets and dust lightly with flour that has been seasoned with salt and pepper. Sauté the chops until golden, turn and place the Proscuitto and cheese on the browned side. Cover the pan and cook for about 5 minutes. Deglaze the pan with white or red wine. If there is oil in the pan, add only as much flour as the oil will absorb and cook and stir for a minute or two before adding wine. Finish by adding a few spoonfuls of half & half or cream to the sauce. Season to taste with salt and pepper and garlic if desired.

Sausage Po Boy

Serves 4

1 pound Italian sausage (hot or sweet as you prefer)
1 loaf French bread (be sure the crust is crisp, heat if necessary)
2 tomatoes, sliced
1 small onion, sliced
1 roasted pepper (see note) or 1 small jar pimentos
1/4 to 1/2 cup extra virgin olive oil

Slice sausage links lengthwise into thirds and remove casings. Fry over medium heat until done. Slice bread lengthwise and scrape out about 1/3 of the soft center. Brush the bread with the olive oil but don't soak it. Put the cooked sausage on the bread and top with the other ingredients. Cut the sandwich into quarters.

<u>Note!</u> *Roast Peppers: Place washed pepper(s) in unsealed plastic bag and place into microwave and cook on high heat for 5-10 minutes. Time will vary as all machines are different. The peppers should be thoroughly wilted. When they reach this point, remove from microwave, in bag, being very careful because they will be very hot. Allow to cool in bag. The skins should remove with ease.*

Special Italian Sausage

Serves 4
1 pound Italian sausage
1 medium onion, diced
1 tablespoon vegetable oil
1 heaping teaspoon garlic, chopped
1/2 cup approximately, red wine
1/4 cup sour cream

Cut sausage in half, lengthwise, and remove skin. Flatten slightly, if desired, to give uniform oblong shape. Heat oil in a skillet and fry sausage over medium heat. When done remove from pan and keep warm. Pour off fat and stir in garlic and onion and sauté until soft. To deglaze, add wine to pan and stir over heat to loosen crispy bits. Add sour cream and stir in thoroughly and season to taste.

Tex-Mex Frittata

Serves 4
1 pound chorizo sausage, Mexican preferred
4 ounces Cheddar or Jack cheese, grated
1 can (4 ounce) diced green chilies, drained
3 green onions, finely sliced
5 large eggs
1 cup milk
1/2 teaspoon salt

Remove casings from sausage and discard them. Sauté the sausage until done, mash sausage while cooking so it is broken into small pieces. Oil a gratin or 9-inch cake pan and put chorizo in bottom. Add remaining ingredients except for eggs, milk and salt. Beat together the eggs, milk and salt and pour over other ingredients. Bake for about 30 minutes or until well browned.

<u>Timesaver Alert!</u> *The word Saltimbocca means literally "Jump in the mouth", and that's what these cutlets do. They are so quick that they jump from the kitchen. You'll love'em*

Pork Cutlets Saltimbocca

Serves 4
8 pork cutlets, about 2 ounces each
8 slices Proscuitto ham
8 sage leaves
1/4 cup flour
3 tablespoons butter
1/2 cup Marsala or Madeira wine
1/4 cup cream

Purchase thinly sliced, boneless pork chops and have the butcher tenderize them TWICE. Use just enough butter to film the bottom of the skillet when butter is melted. Rinse cutlets, lay a slice of Proscuitto on each and tuck Proscuitto edges under to fit on top of cutlet. Place a sage leaf in the center of each Proscuitto slice and use a toothpick as you would a straight pin to fasten the sage to the ham and cutlet. On a plate or sheet of waxed paper spread the flour and lay the bottom side of the cutlet on the flour to give the pork a light dusting of flour. Use a medium size skillet and melt the butter in the skillet until it sizzles and carefully place the meat, sage leaf down, in the butter. Cook for about 2 minutes and turn and cook for about 2 more minutes. Remove the cutlets to a platter and with the heat on high add the wine to the pan and cook until it has begun to reduce. Stir in the cream and check for seasoning. Pour the sauce over the meat and serve at once.

Pork Schnitzel With Shallot And Tomato Sauce

Serves 3 to 4
1 1/2 to 2 cutlets (4 ounces each) per person
1/2 cup all-purpose flour
salt, pepper to taste
3 tablespoons vegetable oil
Shallot and Tomato Sauce, recipe below

Purchase thinly sliced, boneless pork chops, and have the butcher tenderize them. Rinse cutlets. Combine about 1/2 cup flour and about 1/2 teaspoon each salt and black pepper and spread on a sheet of wax paper. Flour the cutlets thoroughly mashing lightly to make a good coating. If time permits, allow the cutlets to rest for about 20 minutes so the flour coating will set. MAKE SAUCE BELOW BEFORE COOKING CUTLETS. Heat the oil until sizzling in a skillet large enough to hold cutlets without crowding. (If necessary cook in two batches.) Sauté the cutlets until well browned, but do not overcook. If necessary add more oil to pan. Serve with noodles.

Shallot And Tomato Sauce

3 to 4 shallots or 1 medium onion, cut in large dice
2 plum tomatoes, cut into large dice
1 tablespoon chopped garlic
3 or 4 sprigs coriander (cilantro), leaves only
2 tablespoons butter
1/4 cup white wine
1/4 cup heavy cream or sour cream
salt and pepper to taste

Over medium heat, melt butter in small skillet and sauté the onion until soft but not brown and add garlic and cook for 1 or 2 minutes. Add tomato and coriander and cook until totally wilted and juicy then add wine and cook for a few minutes until the sauce becomes thick and rather syrupy. Stir in cream and blend thoroughly and season to taste. Keep sauce warm while cooking cutlets.

Poultry

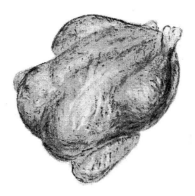

Chicken is almost as versatile as pork, and is more popular. Henry IV became king of France in the 16th Century and promised his people that his goal was "a chicken in every pot". Huey Long, Governor of Louisiana in the 1930's, did much the same, but he upped the ante to "a chicken in every pot, and a car in every garage."

Chicken can be prepared in a host of ways, and each of us has our favorites, but fried tops most lists. What picnic is complete without fried chicken? And how my mother could fry chicken! The best I've ever tasted, and doesn't every child of the south say the same thing?

Chicken is almost interchangeable with veal. The recipes in this chapter present chicken in many ways, some familiar and some more exotic.

The other popular American dinner bird is the turkey. Benjamin Franklin thought the wild turkey, rather than the Bald Eagle, should be the national bird. Turkey might not be as popular as chicken, but what would holiday meals be without it?

Timesaver Alert! The following recipe is a good example of a quick but delightful main dish. It would be delicious with biscuits and country gravy. You can find recipes for those in subsequent chapters of this book.

Note! Goujons are small Mediterranean fish which are fried whole. In this case, goujonettes are pieces of chicken cut roughly the size of goujon and prepared much the same way.

Sautéed Goujonettes of Chicken Breast

Serves 6

2 pounds (more or less) boneless, skinless breast of chicken (or use chicken tenders)
vegetable oil
salt and pepper (about 1 teaspoon of each)
1 teaspoon coarse garlic powder (optional)
about 1 cup flour
about 1 cup buttermilk

Rinse chicken in cool water and drain. On cutting board cut chicken into strips across breast and about 3/4 inch wide (if using tenders no cutting is required). Place strips in mixing bowl and when all are sliced pour buttermilk over and toss to mix. Set knife and cutting board aside and don't use again until thoroughly washed. Place flour, salt and pepper and garlic powder, if used, into a 1 gallon size plastic bag and add chicken about 1/3 at a time (sauté the batch and then 1/3 more in bag, etc. Heat oil 1/2 inch deep in heavy skillet until very hot but not smoking and cook chicken for a minute on a side and then turn. The chicken should cook in 5 minutes or less. When done it feels firm but springy, not hard (too done) or squishy (not done). If cooking in batches, more oil may be needed. Drain chicken on paper towels.

Gourmet & Leftover Alert! *The following recipe is a great example of this new approach to gourmet cooking which can be accomplished in far less time than then the conventional way by using precooked chicken—roasted chicken from the supermarket for example—with no loss in quality. Or use leftovers!*

Chicken with Southern Dumplings

Serves 4 to 6

2 pounds chicken breast or 1 fryer weighing about 3 pounds or 1 cooked and ready to eat whole chicken

1/2 cup diced celery

1/2 cup diced onion

salt and pepper to taste

1 teaspoon chopped fresh sage, or 1/4 teaspoon dry rubbed sage

2 tablespoons chopped parsley

2 quarts purchased chicken broth if using breast or ready to eat chicken

If using chicken breast, place washed breast in a 4-quart pot with lid and cover with about 2 quarts chicken broth bring to boil and simmer for about 20 minutes. Remove from broth and set aside. Season broth to taste with salt and pepper taking care not to over season.

If using raw fryer, wash bird and remove giblets and wash them. Place chicken and giblets in pot with celery and onion add about 2 quarts of water and cover pot. Bring to boil, turn down heat and simmer for about 1 and 1/2 hours. Remove bird and giblets from pot and set them aside to cool, When cool enough to handle remove skin and discard. Remove meat from bones, cut meat into bite-size pieces and discard bones. Season broth to taste with salt and pepper taking care not to over season.

If using cooked chicken, remove skin and bones and cut chicken in bite-size pieces. Season broth to taste with salt and pepper taking care not to over season. Make dumplings, below.

Southern Dumplings

2 cups self-rising flour
1/3 cup soft shortening
1/2 cup milk

Work shortening into flour and add milk gradually to make a stiff dough. Sprinkle lightly with flour and roll out about 1/8 inch thick (a very thin sheet) and cut on the diagonal into diamonds. Dust lightly with flour and drop into boiling broth. Cover pot, lower heat and simmer for about 20 minutes. Remove dumplings to serving bowl, return chicken to broth that should now be somewhat thickened and thicken with buerre manie (see note below) if necessary. When chicken and gravy are thoroughly heated, pour them over dumplings. Sprinkle parsley over top. If you have no parsley, sprinkle lightly with paprika for color. Something tart like pickles or sweet and sour cabbage is a good accompaniment.

Note! *Buerre Manie: Work together equal measures of all-purpose flour and butter until well combined. This mixture will combine with liquids without lumping.*

Leftover Alert! *Again with the cooked chicken! Cacciatora this way is quick and easy even after a hard day's work.*

Quick Cacciatora

Serves 4 to 6
tomato sauce (see below)
2 pounds cooked chicken breast or dark meat, or a combination, skinned, boned and cut into bite size pieces
1 large green bell pepper, seeded and sliced into strips
1 onion about the size of an egg, peeled and sliced in strips from top to root of onion
8 ounces mushrooms, sliced
2 tablespoons extra virgin olive oil

Sauté pepper, onion and mushrooms in olive oil over medium heat in a medium size skillet. When vegetables are wilted but not brown, add chicken and tomato sauce and bring to simmer. Taste for seasoning and if desired add more pesto. Serve over pasta.

Note! *Either of the two sauces below may be used in the Cacciatora above. They are not long simmering sauces, and are just delightful.*

Light Tomato Sauce

Serves 4 to 6
1 large can (1 pound 12 ounce) chopped or crushed tomatoes without seasoning or sugar
2 heaping teaspoons basil pesto, or to taste (commercial is fine)
salt and pepper to taste

Heat tomatoes to light simmer and then season lightly with salt. Add pesto and pepper to taste. This may be served, as is, on pasta or used to make Parmigiana. Or may be used in any dish which requires tomato sauce.

Fresh Tomato Sauce

Serves 4 to 6
2 pounds fresh tomatoes
2 tablespoons butter or extra virgin olive oil if preferred
salt and pepper to taste
fresh basil or basil pesto (commercial is fine) to taste

Skin tomatoes (method follows) and cut into vertical slices or cubes as desired. Melt butter in skillet and add tomatoes. Bring to simmer and season lightly with salt. After salting, add basil or pesto to taste. This sauce may be used in any dish that requires tomato sauce.

Note! *To skin tomatoes: Drop whole tomatoes into a pot of boiling water and remove in about 1 minute into a bowl of cold or ice water. As soon as they are cool enough to handle remove skins and use as desired.*

Breast of Chicken "Cordon Bleu"

Serves 4 to 6
2 pounds boneless, skinless breast of chicken
(more or less)-allow 1 breast half per person plus an extra half or two for leftovers
1 cup, or as needed, all-purpose flour
1 teaspoon salt
1 teaspoon black pepper
3 tablespoons vegetable oil
3 tablespoons butter
salt and black pepper to taste
4 ounces shallots, peeled and sliced
1 tablespoon minced garlic
1 cup dry white wine
1/2 cup cream
1 small or 1/2 large slice Prosciutto ham for each breast half
1 slice Mozzarella cheese, about 2 inches by 4 inches for each breast half

Mix salt and pepper with flour and place in 1 gallon size plastic bag. Divide breast into halves, if necessary, and rinse them under cool water. Flatten breast halves by pounding them gently with mallet or back of heavy knife. It reduces mess and splattering if breasts are placed individually in a plastic bag (not the one with flour) while flattening. Try to flatten breasts to about 1/3 inch at thickest part. Move flattened breasts to separate bag and shake breasts with flour and seasonings. When well floured place breasts on waxed paper for about 15 minutes to allow coating to dry. In skillet large enough to hold chicken without crowding, heat oil and when hot add butter. When butter is beginning to brown slightly add breast pieces and brown, turn and brown other side and then turn again. They should need no longer than 15 minutes to cook. Check by slicing into thickest part of one and if the juices run clear they are done. Remove from pan and make sauce.

To make sauce, pour off all but about 2 tablespoons fat and add shallots. Lightly brown them and then add garlic and cook, for about a minute. Deglaze pan with wine and reduce by boiling for 2 to 3 minutes. Lower heat to medium stir in cream and simmer for 2 to 3 minutes. Salt and pepper to taste.

Top each breast half with Prosciutto and then the cheese and place under broiler until bubbly. Serve with sauce.

<u>Gourmet Alert!</u> *This next recipe will take almost an hour from top to table, but you'll find it well worthwhile. This would be well complemented by a squash side dish or a salad.*

Dijon Chicken

Serves 4
4 large chicken breast halves, skin on, bone in
1 cup all-purpose flour
1 teaspoon each salt and black pepper
4 tablespoons butter
2 tablespoons vegetable oil
1/2 cup Dijon mustard (don't you go using any yellow mustard!)
1/2 cup onion, coarsely chopped
1 tablespoon chopped garlic
salt and pepper
1 cup heavy cream or evaporated milk
1/2 cup dry white wine
Preheat oven to 350°F

Mix flour, salt and pepper in a gallon-size plastic bag. Put chicken in the bag and shake well to flour the chicken. Heat the oil and butter in a skillet until there is a hint of browning, then add chicken and sauté until the chicken is nicely browned, top and bottom. Remove the breasts from the skillet and place them, skin side up, in a gratin or baking dish that has been oiled or sprayed with pan spray. The gratin should be large enough to hold the breasts in one layer. Spread the mustard lightly over the exposed side of the chicken, but do not spread mustard on both sides.

Pour off all but about one tablespoon oil from the skillet and at a moderate temperature sauté the onion until wilted and soft and add garlic and continue to cook for about a minute. Pour the wine into the pan with the onion and garlic and boil, stirring the bits of crust from the bottom. Add the cream and when hot, taste for seasoning and add salt and pepper. Pour the sauce over the chicken breasts and bake for about 30 minutes. The inside temperature of the breasts should be 170° F when done.

Chicken Breast with Shallots

Serves 4 to 6
2 pounds boneless, skinless chicken breasts
2 tablespoons butter
2 large shallots, chopped
salt and pepper
1/2 cup half & half

Divide breasts into two parts, rinse and pat dry. Heat butter in skillet large enough to hold all the pieces. Brown breasts on one side and turn to brown other side and add chopped shallots to skillet. Sauté breasts about 5 minutes per side or until done. Remove breasts, and add half & half. Bring to boil, taste for seasoning and pour over chicken. Serve with pasta or noodles.

<u>**Gourmet Alert!**</u> *This is a wonderful recipe that brings out all the subtle soft flavor of garlic.*

Poulet Mistral

Serves 6
one 3 1/2 to 4 pound chicken
1 teaspoon salt and 1/2 teaspoon black pepper, mixed
2 tablespoons each of butter and olive oil
3 tablespoons all-purpose flour
1 bulb of garlic, divided into cloves and peeled
1 cup red wine
1 cup water
1/2 cup chicken broth
Preheat oven to 400°F

Remove giblets from chicken, wash chicken inside and out and dry skin with paper towels. Sprinkle salt, pepper mix into chicken and tie legs together with kitchen twine for neatness. Oil chicken skin and place in ovenproof pan in which butter has been melted and combined with olive oil. Place chicken in pan on its side and roast for 10 minutes, turn to other side and roast another 10 minutes and then place breast-side down and roast 10 minutes more. While doing initial roasting, blanch garlic for about 10 minutes in about 1 cup of water, reserve water. Reduce heat to 375°F and turn chicken on back for final roasting and add blanched garlic, tossing garlic in the oil in the pan, to coat. The entire roasting time will be about 20 minutes per pound, about 1 1/2 hours. When chicken is cooked and garlic is golden remove from oven, the internal temperature in the thickest part of the thigh should be 180°F. Remove to serving platter and make gravy.

To make gravy, pour off all but about 3 tablespoons oil (save remainder for another use) and stir in flour. Cook for a couple of minutes to rid the flour of its raw taste. Gradually stir in the reserved, strained garlic water and add enough chicken broth and wine to make a nice sauce. Season to taste with salt and pepper.

Timesaver Alert! _See how we keep using cooked chicken to save time? You and your whole family will love the results from this next recipe._

Chicken Vol au Vent

Serves 6
1 package frozen patty shells, baked according to packet directions
1 purchased roasted chicken (1 1/2 to 2 pound)
1/2 cup country ham (or Prosciutto) dice or julienne
1 teaspoon finely chopped garlic
1/2 pound mushrooms, washed and sliced
3 tablespoons butter
2 to 3 tablespoons flour
1 cup (approximately) milk or half & half

Skin chicken, remove meat from bone and cut into 1/2 inch dice. Melt butter in skillet that is large enough for all ingredients. Sauté mushrooms and ham until just beginning to brown, then remove from pan. If necessary, add more butter to make about 3 tablespoons. Cook flour, stirring, for about 2 minutes then whisk or stir in liquid to make a smooth sauce. Season to taste then add chicken, mushrooms and ham. Serve in the baked patty shells.

Easy Repeats

Serves 4 to 6
8 ounces dry pasta, cooked
remainder of Chicken Vol au Vent filling
1 pound packet frozen green peas
extra cream to thin sauce if necessary
grated Parmesan cheese to taste

Heat sauce and add the additional liquid if necessary. Add peas and heat sufficiently to thaw. Serve over pasta with the cheese on side.

Pesto Chicken

Serves 4 to 6
1 pound boneless, skinless chicken breast, sliced into thin strips
1 tablespoon pesto
2 tablespoons extra virgin olive oil
1 summer squash, sliced thinly
1 to 2 tablespoons basil pesto
12 ounces linguini or other long pasta, cooked and kept warm
shredded or grated Parmesan cheese

Toss chicken with 1 tablespoon of olive oil and one of pesto. Heat the remaining olive oil in a skillet and sauté the chicken until lightly golden, being careful not to overcook. The cooking time will be about 5 minutes or less. When done, remove from skillet and quickly sauté the squash slices. Toss the pasta with the remaining pesto using more if desired and toss in chicken and squash. Sprinkle Parmesan over top. Garnish with parsley if desired.

Gourmet & Timesaver Alert! *You won't see a better example of the new method of quick preparation demonstrated in this book than in the next recipe. The chicken tenders, already fried and available at the supermarket, allows you to make this gourmet dish in an unbelievably short time. And will you get the praise!*

Chicken Tenders with Stroganoff Sauce

Served 4 to 6
2 pounds purchased or home fried chicken tenders
Stroganoff Sauce Includes
4 tablespoons butter
3/4 cup slivered onion
12 ounces mushrooms, sliced
2 teaspoons mustard powder
1 tablespoon minced garlic
3 heaping tablespoons flour
1/2 cup chicken broth
1/2 cup, or as needed, half & half
1/2 cup or more, sour cream
salt and pepper to taste

Melt the butter in a large, heavy skillet and when it is sizzling, add mushrooms and sauté, stirring frequently, until they are very nicely browned, about 20 minutes. Add onion to skillet and sauté until wilted and then add flour, stirring in well and cook for about 2 minutes. Add mustard powder and garlic and stir to blend. Add broth and half & half and stir and cook until sauce is nicely formed, then return mushrooms to pan and heat thoroughly. If sauce looks too thick, add more broth and/or half & half. Season to taste with salt and black pepper. Stir in sour cream and heat thoroughly but do not boil.

Serve sauce on the side so chicken remains crisp. This is good with noodles or rice.

Gourmet Alert! *Oyster lovers will be delighted with the next simple and elegant dish. Serve this to guests, and put the oysters in just at the end. You needn't be long away from your guests, but you'd better prepare enough for seconds!*

Chicken with Oysters

Serves 6 to 8
2 pounds chicken thighs, washed
1 cup flour
1 teaspoons each of black pepper and coarse garlic powder
8 ounce container of shelled oysters
1 cup, approximately, half & half or whole milk
4 green onions, sliced
2 tablespoons vegetable oil
12 ounces dry noodles, cooked

Mix flour, salt, pepper and garlic together in a plastic bag. Shake thighs in flour until well coated. Sauté until well browned on both sides. Add onions when browning on second side. When well browned, pour off all possible oil and pour milk over. Turn heat to low medium and cover pan. Cook until done, about 20 minutes. Check oysters for bits of shell. Add oysters and liquid and cover again. Cook until oysters are curling at edges. Taste sauce and adjust seasoning. Serve over noodles.

Gourmet Alert! *Even if you've never tried England's pride and joy, Stilton cheese, you should do yourself a favor and prepare the following recipe. It is a delight and although it requires about an hour to table, it is well worth the time (half of which is while the dish is in the oven and you are free to do other things). This is one every guest will remember.*

Breast of Chicken Stuffed with Stilton

Serves 4
4 boneless, skinless breast halves
4 ounces cream cheese
1/2 cup crumbled Stilton blue cheese
2 green onions, finely chopped
1/2 cup broken walnuts
4 slices bacon
pan spray
Preheat oven to 400°F

Spray thoroughly a gratin or baking dish large enough to hold the breasts lightly touching. In a small bowl, mash the cream cheese and stir in the onion, walnuts and Stilton. Set aside. Lay a slice of bacon on the cutting board and with the flat side of your knife stretch the bacon without tearing it. Working from the long, thick side, slice the breasts almost but not quite through, as though you were butterflying them. Divide the cheese mixture in four parts and form each part in a log long enough to tuck into the breast. Fill all four breasts. Wrap a slice of bacon around each breast and place in baking dish. Spray each breast thoroughly with pan spray. Cook, uncovered, for about 30 minutes, until the juices run clear and the internal temperature is 170°F.

Gourmet & Timesaver Alert! _The next recipe is a wonderful change of pace. It's quick to prepare and your family will think you're a genius. If you try this one please also fix the Spaetzele. You'll be glad you did_

Paprika Chicken

Serves 4

1 boneless, skinless chicken breast half per person, about 4-6 ounces each
1/2 cup all-purpose flour
1 tablespoon chopped garlic
2 teaspoons paprika or to taste, CAUTION: don't use hot paprika
1 medium onion
1 can chicken broth
1/2 cup sour cream
salt and pepper to taste
1 pinch cinnamon, optional
1/4 cup vegetable oil

Put the flour in a plastic bag. Wash the chicken and cut breast halves apart and drop the pieces into the bag with the flour. Shake bag until chicken is well coated. Peel the onion and cut it into half from top to bottom. Slice each half into thin semicircles. Heat the oil in a skillet until very hot but not smoking and add the chicken. Cook until it begins to color, turn and do the same with the other side. Remove the chicken from the pan and set aside. Pour all but 1 tablespoon oil from pan then add the paprika, one tablespoon of the flour left in the bag, the onion and the garlic and cook until the onion has softened and the mixture has a warm, fragrant scent. Pour in the chicken broth and stir to mix. Bring to a boil and simmer for about 5 minutes. Return the chicken to the pan and turn down heat and cook chicken, turning occasionally for about 10 minutes or until done. Add sour cream and stir to blend then salt and pepper to taste. If the sauce tastes a bit "thin" add the pinch of cinnamon. Serve with noodles or spaetzele.

Spaetzele

2 eggs
2 tablespoons vegetable oil
1/2 cup water
1/2 cup milk
2 1/2 cups all-purpose flour
1/2 teaspoon each, salt and pepper
1/2 teaspoon baking powder

Fill a large pot with water, 3 or 4 quarts, and add about 2 teaspoons salt to water. Bring to a boil. Mix all liquids, including eggs, and blend well. Combine dry ingredients and combine with liquids to make a thickish batter. The spaetzele can be cooked by dropping dough by spoonfuls into the boiling water but this will be VERY slow. A spaetzele maker can be made as follows:

Use a coffee can with holes cut in the bottom to hold the raw dough and to press out "Strings" of spaetzele into the boiling water. The holes can be conveniently made in the bottom of the coffee can with a "church key" (one of those old beer can openers that has a triangular knife-like device at the end that you use to puncture tinned milk and other cans of liquid) or use a spoon or colander with large holes through which the batter can be forced.

Cook spaetzele about 5 minutes, and remove from water using a slotted spoon.

Curried Chicken

Serves 4
3 tablespoons butter
2 cups diced onion
2 tablespoons diced garlic
1 tablespoon ginger purée
2 tablespoons Madras curry powder, medium heat
1/4 teaspoon cinnamon
pinch cayenne
1/2 cup golden raisins
1 1/2 cups canned unsweetened coconut milk or as needed
juice of 1/2 lemon
salt to taste
1 pound cooked, diced skinless chicken

In a skillet, heat the butter until it sizzles but is not brown. Stir in the onion and cook, stirring frequently, until it softens then stir in the garlic and ginger. Cook for an additional minute or two then add the curry powder. Cook, stirring, until the mixture gives off a fragrant, spicy smell. Stir in the coconut milk and heat, over medium heat, until the mixture simmers and begins to thicken. Add the raisins, cinnamon and cayenne and add salt to taste. Stir in the lemon juice and again taste for flavor. Stir in the cooked chicken and simmer until well heated through. If mixture looks too thick, add a bit more coconut milk. Serve with rice.

Gourmet & Timesaver Alert! *For most of us southerners, fried foods are particular favorites and we seek new reasons to fry things. Fried chicken has long been a southern favorite and now is a national one. Here is a quick and tasty entry into the chicken lexicon.*

Lime Fried Chicken

Serves 3 to 4

1 1/2 pounds, approximately, chicken breast tenders
1/4 cup fresh lime juice, about 3 limes
1/4 cup Crystal hot sauce
1 tablespoon Worcestershire sauce
1 cup all-purpose flour
2 teaspoons granulated garlic powder
2 teaspoons mild paprika
1 teaspoon black pepper
1 teaspoon salt
1 cup, approximately, vegetable oil.

Combine limejuice, hot sauce and Worcestershire sauce in a bowl large enough to accommodate chicken to marinate. Rinse chicken and place in marinade and marinate, stirring occasionally, for about 1/2 hour at room temperature. In a gallon-size plastic or paper bag, combine all dry ingredients and shake to blend. Pour oil into a skillet large enough to fry 1/2 of the chicken at a time. The oil should be about 1/4 inch deep. When chicken has marinated, remove chicken from liquid and drop into the bag of flour and seasonings. Shake to cover each piece thoroughly. Heat the oil very hot but not smoking and place chicken pieces, not touching, into the hot oil. The tenders are small enough that when they are well browned on both sides they are cooked.

Note! *This is a deep south country dish, and there is nothing Italian about it. When I was a teen it seemed like every housewife had her own special recipe for it. Pesto is my addition; basil was unknown in the rural south until recently. For me, this is a comfort food.*

Chicken and Spaghetti

Serves 6

1 pound cooked chicken, cut into small dice (you can purchase a roasted chicken)
2 tablespoons extra virgin olive oil
2 ribs celery
1 medium onion
1/2 bell pepper, optional
2 tablespoons finely chopped garlic
2 tablespoons purchased basil pesto
1 can (28 ounce) diced tomatoes in juice
1/4 teaspoon crushed red pepper
8 ounces (raw weight) spaghetti, cooked
6 ounces sharp Cheddar cheese, grated
salt
Preheat oven to 350°F

Dice the celery, onion and pepper into small pieces and sauté until wilted in the olive oil. Add the garlic and crushed red pepper and cook for an additional minute. Stir in the tomato and pesto and cook for about 15 minutes. Salt to taste and add chicken and heat thoroughly. Combine in an oiled baking dish large enough to hold everything, the sauce, spaghetti and cheese. Toss to combine. If all ingredients, including pasta are hot, then bake until cheese is melted. If all ingredients aren't hot then bake for about 45 minutes or until bubbly, and cheese is lightly browned.

Gourmet Alert! *Try as you might to avoid it, there will probably come a time when you feel obliged to fix a holiday dinner of turkey and fixin's. The recipes that follow are as easy and as delicious as can be devised to help pull you through that day. Who knows, you might even grow to like doing this sort of thing!*

Roast Turkey

Serves 4 to 6 with leftovers
approximately 12 pound turkey
1 tablespoon each salt and black pepper
1 tablespoon dried rosemary or 2 large sprigs fresh
2 tablespoons coarse granulated garlic
pan spray
preheat oven to 350°F

Thoroughly thaw turkey in refrigerator or under running water. NEVER THAW AT ROOM TEMPERATURE. Thawing time is given on turkey package. When thawed, remove structure that secures legs.

To make broth remove neck, tail and giblets and put them in a pan, cover with water and simmer covered until done, at least 1 hour. Meanwhile, rinse turkey and pat dry. Line a roasting pan with foil and place a low rack in pan. Spray the rack thoroughly with pan spray. Mix the seasonings and sprinkle all of them in cavity. Tie legs together with butcher twine. Spray turkey all over the skin with pan spray. Put turkey on the rack, breast side down. Cover bird with foil and secure edges of foil under the edges of the pan. Place in oven. Roast approximately 2 hours then remove from oven, remove foil and turn turkey so breast side is up. Roast uncovered (still on rack) approximately 2 more hours or until turkey is nicely browned and the internal temperature of thigh is 180°F. The pop-up guide will react at about this point. Remove turkey from roaster to platter and let rest while making gravy.

Gravy

3 to 4 tablespoons pan drippings from the turkey roaster pan
equal amount by measure of flour
salt, pepper and granulated garlic to taste
chicken or turkey broth
1/2 cup dry white wine

Make gravy in roaster pan by pouring off all fat but about 3 tablespoons. Place roaster over medium heat on top of stove and stir in about 3 tablespoons of flour or until no fat is showing. Cook stirring for about 5 minutes. Stir in enough wine and broth to make gravy of desired consistency. Bring to a boil and then simmer gravy for 2 to 3 minutes. Taste for seasoning and add salt, pepper, and granulated garlic to taste.

Fancied-up Cranberry Sauce

8 to 10 servings
1-1 pound can whole berry cranberry sauce
1/4 cup orange marmalade
Combine above ingredients and serve.

Basic Cornbread Dressing

8 to 10 servings
8 cups crumbled cornbread (recipe follows)
6 cups crumbled bread (see below)*
1 large onion, about 1 cup chopped
4 spears celery, diced
1 quart chicken or turkey broth
salt and black pepper to taste
3 tablespoons chopped parsley
3 tablespoons chopped fresh sage or
1 to 2 teaspoons dried sage or to taste
2 large eggs

Simmer celery and onion in broth about 1/2 hour or until soft. Pour off broth to measure and add water to bring the amount back to 1 quart. Put broth, and cooked seasonings into large bowl. Crumble in corn bread.

*Put about 1 pound loaf of white bread (stale bread is best) in a separate bowl and cover with water. When bread is soaked, squeeze out water and measure bread. Add squeezed-out bread to broth, seasonings, and cornbread and stir to mix. Salt and pepper and season with parsley and sage to taste. When seasoned to satisfaction, add eggs and stir in. Place in large, greased baking pan and bake at 350° F for approximately 1 1/2 hours or until 170°F in center of pan.

To this basic dressing, before cooking one of the following could be added:
  1 pound pork sausage, cooked and crumbled
  1/2 pounds of roasted peeled and chopped chestnuts
  1 pound sliced and sautéed mushrooms
  1 quart chopped oysters and liquid

Cornbread

enough for dressing above
3 cups self-rising cornmeal
1 1/2 cups buttermilk
3 tablespoons vegetable oil
3 large eggs
one 9-inch oven proof skillet
2 tablespoons oil
Preheat oven to 400°F

Swirl oil around skillet and heat until sizzling (hot but not smoking) in oven or on top of stove. Combine all ingredients and place in hot skillet. Bake approximately 30 minutes or until done. This is a wonderful, light cornbread and can be made with the proportions of 1 cup meal, 1 egg, 1/2 cup buttermilk and 1 tablespoon oil.

Note! *The chili below is as good as any I've tasted—even though it is turkey. Try it you'll like it. The trick is that there is so much seasoning, that you can't tell its turkey!*

Turkey Chili

serves 4 to 6
1 package, 1 1/4 pounds, approximately, ground turkey
2 tablespoons vegetable oil
1 small onion, finely diced
1 heaping teaspoon granulated garlic
1/4 cup chili powder
1 can (28 ounce) tomato purée
1/2 cup finely chopped fresh coriander (cilantro)
salt to taste

In a heavy, approximately 3 quart pot with lid, sauté the onion, turkey and chili powder, stirring frequently until the turkey is cooked. Add the tomato purée and garlic and bring to light boil and immediately lower heat to low and simmer for about 15 minutes. Salt to taste and if the chili tastes "flat" add a bit more garlic. Stir in the coriander. Cover and simmer for an additional 15 minutes. Taste for salt.

Seafood

In the 50's when I was a teenager, it seemed that families interacted more on social occasions than they do today. Fish fries were popular local entertainment, and the food was wonderful. Huge iron pots, originally designed to boil clothes in to wash them — but that's a different story — were filled with lard and placed on brick barbecue pits. A roaring fire was built under them, and the fat was heated to a rolling boil. Catfish and plump hush puppies were fried. The catfish were wild, caught in the Mississippi River or at one of the local horseshoe lakes, left behind years before by the river's meandering. The fish were full of flavor and huge, some weighing 20 or more pounds. The hush puppies were always made with white cornmeal. They were bursting with onion, but not a grain of sugar in them! Cole slaw and white bread were always accompaniments. Dessert would be homemade ice cream and cake. With memories like that, I grew up loving fish and the occasions for eating fish.

Nowadays, we prepare fish and shell fish in more and fancier ways, but I suspect we would have less trouble getting children to eat fish if they were enjoying it with friends, on a fall evening with frost in the air, and the delicious aroma of dinner tantalizing them.

Tuna and Artichoke Pie

Serves 4 to 6
3 large eggs
2 cans (6 1/2 ounce each) solid pack tuna in oil, drained
1 jar marinated artichoke hearts, drained
(save marinade for use in a salad dressing)
1 cup sour cream
grated zest and juice of 1 lemon
1/2 teaspoon salt
1/2 teaspoon black pepper
1 heaping tablespoon chopped parsley
1 deep dish 9-inch pie shell (purchased frozen will do nicely)
Preheat oven to 350°F

Bake pie shell until lightly golden, about 10 minutes, and cool before adding remainder of ingredients. Beat together eggs, sour cream, lemon zest and juice, salt and pepper. Place 1/2 the artichoke hearts on bottom of pie shell then 1/2 the tuna. Repeat with remainder. Pour the cream-egg mixture over and sprinkle with parsley. Bake for about 40 minutes or until puffed and golden.

Gourmet & Timesaver Alert! *This is a delightful recipe all fish lovers will go for. Of course, it's the marinade that makes the dish, but whatever it is, this will be a favorite in your house for many years.*

Salmon Nuggets

Serves 4 to 6
1 1/2 pounds fresh salmon filet
3 tablespoons soy sauce (regular not "lite")
3 tablespoons orange juice
1 teaspoon grated fresh ginger
1 tablespoon butter

Remove skin from salmon and cut the fish into pieces about 1/2 inch by 1 inch. In a bowl large enough to hold the salmon without crowding, combine the soy, orange juice and ginger, and stir to blend. Put the salmon pieces into the marinade and toss gently to coat with marinade. Refrigerate and marinate for about 10 minutes. When ready to cook, heat the butter until it sizzles in a skillet large enough to hold salmon easily. Place salmon pieces in skillet and reserve marinade. Cook salmon until golden, being careful not to overcook. The cooking time will be about 3 to 4 minutes. When done, remove fish from skillet and pour off oil. Add the marinade to the pan and bring to a boil and pour over salmon. This dish is best with unassertive dishes such as butter braised cabbage and a lemon couscous.

Note! George Clark was the snack bar cook at Henson Creek Golf Course. George was my inspiration for salmon cakes and black pepper biscuits, found in the "Breads and Such" Chapter later in this book. Using Cheez-its is my twist on his recipe. They add lots of good flavor.

Simply Delicious Salmon Cakes

Serves 4 to 6

2 cans (14.75 ounce each) salmon or about 1 1/2 pounds cooked fresh salmon
1/2 cup finely diced green or bulb onion
1/2 cup finely diced bell pepper or celery
3/4 cup Cheez-its cracker crumbs
1/2 to 1 cup mayonnaise
salt, pepper and hot sauce to taste
2 large eggs
vegetable oil

Drain salmon (if using canned) crumble and remove skin and bones. Combine with next three ingredients and blend thoroughly. Add enough mayonnaise to moisten the mixture well. More mayonnaise will be necessary if you are using cooked fresh salmon. Season to taste with salt, pepper and hot sauce before adding eggs. Stir in eggs and form the mixture into cakes about 2 1/2 inches in diameter and about 1/2 inch or less thick. Heat a skillet and cover the bottom lightly with vegetable oil. Sauté the cakes until well browned and then turn and brown the other side. Cook until cakes feel firm. Repeat until all the mix is cooked, keeping the cooked cakes warm in the oven. Serve with lemon wedges.

Dinner Bruschetta

Serves 6

6 thick slices, Italian or sour dough bread, approximately 1/2 inch thick, cut on the diagonal
6 to 7 tablespoons extra virgin olive oil
1/2 teaspoon garlic purée
2 medium tomatoes or 1 large, finely diced
1 avocado, peeled and diced
2 cans (6.5 ounce each) white tuna, preferably oil pack, drained
juice 1/2 lemon
salt and pepper to taste

Gently toss together the tuna, tomato, avocado, lemon juice and 2 to 3 tablespoon olive oil. Season to taste with salt and pepper. Set aside. Toast bread and lightly brush with a mixture of 4 tablespoon olive oil mixed with the garlic. Divide the tuna mixture and pile on the toasted bread. This is great with a soup such as gazpacho.

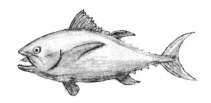

Salmon Kedgeree

Serves 4 to 6

2 tablespoons medium Madras curry paste or 2 tablespoons mild curry powder
1 teaspoon ginger purée
1 cup chopped onion, shallot or spring onion
1 cup uncooked frozen green peas
2 tablespoons vegetable oil
3 cups cooked white rice
1 pound, approximately, cooked fresh salmon, broken into bite-size pieces juice of 1 lemon
salt and pepper to taste

Heat oil in a medium skillet over medium heat until it is hot but not smoking and sauté the onion until soft but not brown, then add curry paste or powder and cook for 1 or 2 minutes, add ginger and cook for another minute. Add salmon and cook until totally heated then add peas and cook for about 3 minutes until they are thawed and hot. Stir in lemon juice and blend thoroughly with rice mixture. Then season to taste. Good as a brunch dish with scrambled eggs and a fruit salad, or for lunch or dinner with a salad.

Gourmet & Timesaver Alert! *Another recipe that is extremely fast and just delightful. Try it and see!*

Shrimp Provençal

Serves 3 to 4
1 pound raw shrimp, peeled
1 small onion or shallot, chopped
2 green onions, sliced thinly into rings
1/4 cup chopped parsley
1 small tomato, plum or salad, chopped
1 heaping tablespoon chopped garlic
4 tablespoons butter
juice 1/2 lemon
dash of Tabasco

In skillet, melt butter, not allowing it to get too hot, add vegetables and garlic and sauté until soft. Add shrimp and cook until pink, stirring frequently. Add salt and Tabasco to taste and finally squeeze in lemon juice. Serves 4 as a sauce for pasta, serves 3 as a main course. Warm French bread to sop up juices is a must.

Pesto Prawns

Serves 4
1 pound medium to large raw shrimp, peeled
3 green onions
1 tablespoon vegetable oil and 1 tablespoon butter or
2 tablespoons butter
2 tablespoons or to taste, basil pesto (homemade or purchased)
1 tablespoon capers, drained
1/4 teaspoon crushed red pepper or a dash of cayenne
1 teaspoon peeled fresh ginger, finely diced or grated
1/2 cup whipping cream
salt and black pepper to taste
12 ounces pasta, cooked

Wash and slice the green onions and sauté in 1/2 of the fat which has been heated to sizzling. Cook until soft but not brown. Remove from pan and set aside. Reheat pan and add remainder of fat and bring to sizzling and add shrimp and cook until pink and curled. Don't overcook. Return onion to pan and add the capers, pesto, ginger and hot pepper. Stir all together and cook for a minute or two. Add cream, stir together and taste for seasoning. Serve over pasta or rice.

Gourmet Alert! *If I have a favorite in the book this may have to be it. It is not only delightful to the palate, but it is beautiful as well. I developed this recipe for a bride who wanted a dish that was pink and had no garlic. How's that for specifications! If you don't try another recipe in the book, do try this one!*

Shrimp Aurora

Serves 4
4 shallots, finely chopped
3 tablespoons butter
3 tablespoons flour
tomato purée (about 1/2 cup)
1/2 heavy cream
1/2 cup white wine
1 pound peeled cooked shrimp

Melt the butter in a medium skillet and sauté the shallots until soft then stir in flour and cook for about 2 minutes, stirring frequently. Add wine and simmer for about 2 minutes then stir in cream and tomato purée. Heat thoroughly and season to taste with salt and pepper then add shrimp and heat thoroughly. Serve over pasta or rice.

Note! *There are no snails in this recipe. But the garlic butter that is used to flavor the shrimp is the same as is traditionally used for snails.*

Shrimps with Snail Butter

Serves 3 generously
1 1/4 pounds raw shrimp, peeled
4 tablespoon Snail Butter (recipe below)

Heat Snail Butter until melted. CAUTION: DURING THE WHOLE PROCESS COOK AT LOW ENOUGH TEMPERATURE TO KEEP THE BUTTER FROM OVERHEATING AND BECOMING OILY. Cook shrimp just until pink and curled.

Snail Butter

1 stick butter at room temperature
1 large or 2 small cloves garlic, finely diced
2 shallots, finely diced
1/4 cup finely diced parsley

Combine all ingredients thoroughly and salt to taste.

Charleston Shrimp

Serves 6

approximately 4 ounces bacon, use smoky slab bacon if available, thick-sliced will do as a substitute
1 large ripe tomato, coarsely diced
1 medium onion, peeled and diced
1 teaspoon finely chopped garlic
2 tablespoons all-purpose flour
1 tablespoon mild hot sauce, such as Crystal
3/4 cup cream or half & half
12 to 16 ounces cooked peeled small to medium shrimp
salt to taste

Dice the bacon. If using slab bacon, remove the rind before frying. When bacon is crisp, remove from skillet and drain on paper towels. Pour off all but about 3 tablespoons fat from skillet. In the reserved fat, sauté, at medium temperature, the onion until soft then add garlic and flour and cook for about 2 minutes. Add tomato and cook for about 2 minutes. Stir in cream or half & half and hot sauce. Cook, stirring, until a nice sauce is formed. It should be thick. Add the shrimp and cook for about 5 minutes or until the shrimp are heated thoroughly. The juice from the shrimp will help thin the sauce. Salt to taste. Serve with grits. (see Vegetable Chapter)

Eggs and Cheese

When I was a child and my mother sent me to the store to buy a dime's worth of cheese, I didn't need to ask her what kind to get. The only cheese available was cheddar or "rat cheese" as it was called. The wheel of cheese was kept on the store counter under a screen cover. I would tell Mr. Thomas what I wanted and he would take a large cheese cutter and cut a nice wedge. The cheddar was bright gold, and was really very good.

When we went to Jackson to shop, my daddy, who loved cheese, bought cheeses that seemed incredibly exotic: Swiss, blue and even Limburger. I sampled and enjoyed (except for the Limburger—I could never get past the smell) but cheddar remained my favorite, as it is to this day. It is an all around cheese, wonderful for use in appetizers to desserts. Melted over apple pie it is divine.

With a wedge of cheese, some eggs and milk a meal is always possible.

The recipes in this chapter give a tantalizing peek at the wonders of cheese and eggs. Enjoy!

Chili Con Queso

one 2 pound package of processed cheese
1 can Ro-tel tomatoes

Place the contents of the can of tomatoes in a non-reactive pan (don't use aluminum or copper) and chop the cheese into cubes about the size of ice cubes. Melt over low heat, stirring often, it burns easily. Use as a dip with chips, to make nachos, on hamburgers and as a topping for vegetables.

Stacked Cheese Enchiladas

Serves 4
1 package corn tortillas
1 can Ro-tel tomatoes
1 cup shredded Cheddar or Jack cheese
1 cup chopped green onion
oil for frying
Preheat oven to 350°F

To fry, use a small skillet, just a little larger than the tortillas. Pour in oil to a depth of about 1/4 inch and heat to hot but not smoking. Fry tortillas, one at a time, until limp and blistered. Drain on paper towels. For baking, use a shallow, ungreased, baking dish, roughly 1 1/2 to 2 inches wider than the tortillas. Put a film of tomato, from the can of tomato, in the bottom of the baking dish and lay in the first tortilla. Sprinkle the tortilla with a tablespoon each of sauce, cheese and onion. Continue with the remainder of tortillas. If any tomato, cheese or onion is left, just pour it on the top. A wooden skewer can be inserted down the middle of the stack to keep the tower from slipping. Bake uncovered for 15 to 20 minutes, or until cheese is melted. Cut in wedges.

Note! *This was a popular dish in the 20's and 30's when chafing dish cookery was fashionable. It is worth reviving because it makes an easy and delicious brunch.*

Goldenrod Eggs

Serves 4 to 6
2 hard boiled eggs per person
double recipe White Sauce with Cheese
salt, pepper, nutmeg and cayenne pepper to taste

Boil, cool and peel eggs. Cut egg white into small pieces and stir into hot sauce. Toast 2 slices bread per person and cut into triangles and put on plates. Pour sauce over toast and sieve yolk over.

White Sauce with Cheese

2 cups whole milk or half & half
2 tablespoons butter
3 tablespoons flour
salt and pepper
nutmeg or garlic or cayenne or herbs to taste
1 cup grated Cheddar cheese

Melt butter over low to moderate heat in a heavy saucepan, stir in flour and cook, stirring all the while, for about 2 minutes to eliminate the raw taste of the flour, but the butter must not be allowed to brown. Pour in the milk and bring to a gentle boil, whisking to incorporate the liquid and make a smooth, silky sauce. Lower heat to a simmer, whisking often, to reduce to the desired thickness. Season to taste with salt and desired seasoning and/or cheese.

For a Velouté Sauce for fish or chicken, substitute rich chicken broth for half the milk, and omit the cheese.

Gourmet Alert! *This is the southern version of Macaroni and Cheese; it has no white sauce in it. It is a recipe right out of my childhood, and is probably among my top ten favorites in the book*

Baked Macaroni and Cheese

Serves 4 to 6
8 ounces elbow macaroni or other similarly sized pasta
1 can (12 ounce) evaporated whole milk
8 ounces sharp or extra sharp Cheddar cheese, grated
2 eggs
1 teaspoon salt, 1 teaspoon black pepper
1 teaspoon Worcestershire sauce
dash of Tabasco (optional)
Preheat oven to 350°F

Cook the pasta according to package directions until tender but not soft and drain thoroughly. Spray with pan spray a baking dish that will hold about 2 quarts. I prefer one which is rather shallow so there will be plenty of crisp top. Beat the eggs and combine with the milk and seasonings. Barely cover the bottom of the baking dish with a bit of the milk mixture and then make a layer of half the pasta, then a layer of half the grated cheese, layer with the remaining pasta and cover the top with the remaining cheese. Pour the milk mixture over all. Bake for about 30 minutes or until firm and golden (internal temperature 170°F).

Note! *I like the taste of Egg Foo Yong but often I've found the restaurant version unbearably greasy. To add insult to injury the accompanying sauce is likely to be a glutinous mess. I experimented and here is the result. It's not greasy or glutinous and it's quite tasty.*

Shrimp Egg Foo Yong

Serves 4
6 eggs
1 small packet (6 ounce size) frozen salad shrimp or equal amounts of pork, chicken, etc.
1 cup thinly sliced vegetables, cabbage, broccoli, bean sprouts, whatever
1/2 cup green onion, thinly sliced
1 tablespoon butter or oil
1 teaspoon soy sauce

If using frozen shrimp, thaw and drain then squeeze lightly in a paper towel. Heat the butter or oil in a non-stick skillet and sauté shrimp or meat with the vegetables, onion and soy sauce until the vegetables are wilted. Remove from skillet and drain thoroughly. Beat eggs well and add the sautéed ingredients and stir to mix. Wipe the skillet dry and oil, or spray with pan spray and heat until hot but not smoking. Dip the egg mix by tablespoons and fry like pancakes, cooking them until well browned on each side. Keep warm while cooking the remainder. Serve at once with sauce on next page.

Egg Foo Yong Sauce

1/2 cup soy sauce
3 tablespoons plum jelly or jam (purchased at supermarket)
a few drops of sesame oil
chopped fresh coriander (cilantro) or green onion

Combine soy and plum jelly and heat in a small sauce pan on low heat until jelly is melted. Add sesame a drop or two at a time, stirring after each addition until it is to your taste. Remove from heat, put in serving dish and sprinkle with coriander or onion.

<u>Note!</u> *Is there a comfort food quicker and easier than a grilled cheese sandwich? Use good cheese and bread and it will be extra good. If desired, add a couple of slices of crisp bacon and a slice of ripe tomato.*

Grilled Swiss Cheese on Sourdough or Rye Bread

2 slices bread per person
sliced Swiss cheese
butter
mustard (not honey mustard)

Assemble sandwiches. In a non-stick skillet or one lightly sprayed with pan spray, sauté the sandwiches on one side until the bread is crisp and golden. Carefully turn them and cook the other side until golden and the cheese is melted. Serve at once.

Quiche with Bacon, Cheese and Green Onion

Serves 4
1 purchased deep 9-inch pie shell
3 large eggs
1/2 pound sliced bacon
1/2 cup cheese, Cheddar, Brie or Swiss
4 green onions with tops
1 1/2 cups whole milk or half & half
1/4 teaspoon salt
1/2 teaspoon black pepper
Preheat oven to 375°F

Bake pie shell at 375°F for about 6 minutes, do not brown, remove from oven. Lower heat to 350°F. Cut bacon into dice and fry crisp and drain on paper towels. Grate the cheese. If using brie, remove the crust and cut cheese into small cubes. Wash the green onion and cut into 1-inch pieces. Whisk the eggs lightly then add milk or half & half and the salt and pepper. Distribute the bacon, cheese and onion evenly in the piecrust and pour the milk mixture over. Bake on a foil-lined baking pan for about 50 minutes or until quiche is puffed and brown.

Pasta

Over the course of the last few years there has been a virtual explosion of pasta preparation in this country. It appears to be a favorite base for sauces. In keeping with the thrust of this book, pasta dishes are almost universally quick to prepare, and with a little care in the application of herbs can be flavorful and filling.

Most brands of pasta sold at your local supermarket will be acceptable. Their flavors will not be very different from one another, but you should look carefully at the type of wheat used in making the pasta. For a good firm texture pick a brand made from hard durum Semolina wheat. Those made from summer wheat will be limp, and soft, rather like noodles. In general, you will find that most of the Italian brands will be durum Semolina, and the U.S. brands are more likely to be soft summer wheat. This is rather a strange situation, in that most of the durum semolina is grown here and shipped to Italy.

Pasta with Ham and Spinach

Serves 4

8 ounces pasta
4 ounces country ham or Prosciutto, sliced in julienne
1 cup grated Parmesan or Romano cheese, not packed
1/2 pound leaf spinach, fresh or frozen
4 or 5 tablespoons butter cut into bits
salt and pepper to taste

Cook pasta in boiling water. If frozen spinach is used, drop it into pasta and boiling water for about 1 minute then drain together. Add butter. If using fresh spinach, do not boil, but rinse it thoroughly, drain and toss with hot pasta and butter. In any case mix in ham julienne and lastly cheese. Toss to mix. Season to taste. You probably will not need salt. Serve immediately.

Pasta with Creamy Sauce

Serves 6 to 8
1 large or 2 medium onions, peeled, quartered and sliced
1 heaping teaspoon chopped garlic
2 to 4 tablespoons extra virgin olive oil (if using sausage use only 2, if not use 4 for flavor)
1/4 teaspoon crushed red pepper
1/4 cup (about) chopped fresh parsley
4 small sprigs fresh rosemary, chopped
1 can (28 ounce) crushed tomatoes (unflavored)
1 pound of fettuccine or linguini, cooked until just done
1 cup whole milk ricotta cheese
1 pound Italian sausage, peeled and cooked and broken into pieces (optional)
parsley for garnish

Sauté the onion, garlic, red pepper and herbs in the oil in a skillet large enough to hold all ingredients, including the pasta, and attractive enough to go to table. Cook until soft, stirring occasionally. Add the tomatoes and cook over low heat for about 15 minutes. If using sausage, add at this point and stir to coat with sauce. Add about 3/4 of the ricotta and stir gently to blend. Add pasta and dot with the remaining ricotta. Sprinkle with parsley for garnish.

Pasta with Ham and Asparagus

Serves 4
8 to 12 ounces pasta, cooked
1 cup ham julienne
1 cup fresh asparagus (6 to 8 spears) cut into diagonals about 1/2 inch long
3 tablespoons butter
1/2 cup grated or shredded Parmesan cheese

Cook pasta and keep hot. Melt butter and sauté ham and asparagus until heated through. Toss with pasta and finally toss in cheese.

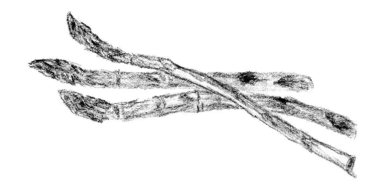

Pasta with Asparagus and Snail Butter

Serves 4

1/2 pound pasta, any shape
1/2 pound fresh asparagus
4 tablespoons Snail Butter (see recipe below)
Parmesan or Romano cheese if desired

Cut asparagus in 1-inch pieces. Cook pasta and during the last 2 minutes of cooking add asparagus to pot to cook. Remove pasta and asparagus to bowl and toss with Snail Butter, and cheese if desired.

Snail Butter

1 stick butter at room temperature
1 large or 2 small cloves garlic, finely diced
2 shallots, finely diced
1/4 cup finely diced parsley

Combine all ingredients thoroughly and salt to taste.

Gourmet Alert! This recipe is just delicious. The combination of the three cheeses makes this one unique.

French Bistro Macaroni

Serves 4
1/2 pound elbow macaroni
about 3/4 pound cooked ham, cut in julienne
1 mild onion or 4 green onions, cut into small pieces, do not use a strong onion
1 1/2 cups ricotta
1 1/2 cups whole milk
salt, pepper and Tabasco to taste
1/4 cup grated or shredded Parmesan cheese
8 ounces Gruyére cheese, diced or grated
Preheat oven to 425°F

Cook the macaroni until it has started to swell, but is still quite hard, drain. Mix macaroni with the ham, ricotta and milk and season to taste.

Make the seasoning rather assertive. Spray a shallow casserole with pan spray and add the prepared mixture. Sprinkle on the cheeses. Bake for about 25 minutes or until nicely browned and the liquid is absorbed. Let sit for a few minutes before serving.

Lemon and Butter Pasta

Serves 4
zest and juice of 1 lemon
3 medium summer squash, thinly sliced
2 ounces butter (1/2 stick)
12 ounce corkscrew or gemelli pasta, cooked

In a skillet, large and nice enough to hold all the pasta and go to table, sauté the squash in the butter, gently so as not to brown the butter. When squash is cooked but still crisp, add pasta and toss to mix well with the butter. Add the lemon juice and zest and toss again. This is a good side dish with simply prepared salmon or beef. Do not use zucchini, they have too much moisture.

Pasta with Eggplant and Tomato

Serves 4 to 6
1 large eggplant
Parmesan cheese
1 can (28 ounce) tomato purée
2 tablespoons chopped garlic
1/4 cup extra virgin olive oil
1/2 teaspoon, or to taste, crushed red pepper
12 ounces dry pasta, cooked
Preheat oven to 350°F

Cut eggplant in thickish chunks, do not peel, and place on greased (or pan-sprayed) foil lined baking pan. Brush eggplant with oil or spray with pan spray. Bake until lightly browned. Cook pasta and set aside. Make Pasta Sauce below.

Pasta Sauce

Use a skillet large enough to hold the sauce and the pasta when it is added just before serving. Put oil, garlic, red pepper and 1/2 teaspoon salt in skillet and heat on low for 2 to 3 minutes or until garlic begins to turn golden, add tomato and allow to simmer for 15 minutes until sauce is well blended. Salt to taste and add pasta and eggplant to sauce. Toss gently and allow pasta and eggplant to rest in sauce for a couple of minutes to absorb sauce. Serve in pasta or soup plates.

Chicken and Eggplant Pasta

Serves 4
1/2 pound raw boneless, skinless chicken breast, cut into julienne
1/2 pound eggplant
3 tablespoons extra virgin olive oil
1/2 pound pasta, cooked
Parmesan cheese to taste
Parsley, optional, to garnish

Wash eggplant and cut off stem end but do not peel. Cut lengthwise then cut into strips lengthwise then crosswise into about 1/2 inch dice. In a skillet, large enough to hold all ingredients, heat the olive oil and sauté the chicken until done, about 4 minutes. Remove chicken and reserve. Sauté the eggplant until slightly softened without adding more oil to pan. Stir or shake pan often to keep eggplant from burning. Return chicken to pan and add pasta. Toss together and sprinkle with Parmesan and parsley. If it seems dry, a bit more oil may be added.

Eggplant and Pasta Gratin

Serves 4

1 large, firm eggplant, (see below)
1/2 pound pasta, cooked and hot
Arrabbiata sauce, see below
1 cup, approximately, shredded Parmesan cheese
salt and pepper to taste
chopped fresh parsley, optional
Preheat oven to 350°F

Oil or spray with pan spray, a gratin large enough to contain all ingredients (about 2 quart size). Lightly cover the bottom of the baking dish with tomato sauce and then make a layer of pasta then a layer of eggplant, continue until all ingredients are used, making sure to finish with eggplant. Sprinkle top thickly with Parmesan cheese. Bake for about 25 minutes, until bubbly and top is golden.

To Prepare Eggplant

Preheat oven to 350°F

Slice eggplant into rounds about 1/3 inch thick DO NOT PEEL. Spray a foil covered cookie sheet with pan spray and place eggplant slices on the foil. Spray tops of slices. Bake until slices are lightly browned. DO NOT TURN THEM. Remove from oven. The eggplant can be cooked and refrigerated a day or two before using.

Arrabbiata Sauce

Serves 6

1/4 cup virgin or extra virgin olive oil
2 tablespoons chopped garlic
1/2 teaspoon crushed red pepper
salt to taste
1 can (28 ounce) crushed tomatoes

Put oil, garlic, red pepper and 1/2 teaspoon salt in a heavy 2 quart pot or skillet and heat on low for 2 to 3 minutes or until garlic begins to turn golden. Add tomato and allow to simmer for 15 minutes until sauce is well blended. Salt to taste.

Pasta with Hot Italian Sausage

Serves 4

1 pound hot (not sweet) Italian sausage, peeled and sliced
2 tablespoons extra virgin olive oil
1 large onion
8 ounces mushrooms, sliced
1 tablespoon chopped garlic
1 cup fresh or canned chopped tomato
1 tablespoon chopped parsley
1/2 pound pasta, cooked

In a heavy 3-quart saucepan with lid, sauté the sausage, covered, in the olive oil until about half cooked. If necessary, pour off excess oil, leaving about 2 tablespoons. Peel the onion and slice in half lengthwise and then into thin semicircles. Add the onion and mushrooms to the sausage and cook until wilted and starting to brown then add the garlic and cook for a minute or two. Add the tomatoes and re-cover the pan. Cook for about 5 minutes then taste for seasoning and add salt and pepper if desired. If the sauce tastes a bit thin add about 1/2 cup dry red wine and allow to simmer for about 5 minutes. Add the pasta to the sauce and allow to heat gently for about 5 minutes. Just before serving, add parsley.

Beef and Saga Blue Pasta

Serves 4
1/2 pound linguini or other pasta, cooked
6 ounces, approximately, of Saga Blue cheese cut into small cubes
1/2 pound of beef tenderloin tip or sirloin, sliced into slivers
parsley or slivers of green onion
2 tablespoons butter

Cook pasta and set aside to keep warm. Sauté the beef to desired doneness and if the skillet is very hot add a portion of the pasta to cushion the cheese from intense heat. Toss the meat, cheese and pasta until the cheese is melted then add the remainder of the pasta and toss all together. Transfer to serving dish and serve at once.

Pasta with Beef and Mushrooms

Serves 4
2 tablespoons butter
1/2 pound sirloin or other tender beef, cut into small pieces
6 medium mushrooms, about 1/3 pound, sliced
1 rounded teaspoon chopped garlic
1/2 cup dry red wine
1/2 cup heavy cream
salt and pepper to taste
8 ounces pasta, cooked

Cook pasta and set aside to keep warm. In a skillet large enough to hold all the ingredients, including pasta, sauté the mushrooms and garlic briefly in the butter then add beef and cook to desired doneness Add the wine and simmer for about 2 minutes. Add cream and simmer briefly, stirring to blend. Taste for seasoning and add salt and pepper to taste. Toss in drained cooked hot pasta.

Pasta with Hot Italian Sausage and Winter Squash

Serves 4
1 package, about 1 pound hot Italian sausage
1 large acorn or small butternut squash, roughly 1 pound
2 tablespoons butter
1 teaspoon salt
8 ounces pasta, cooked
1/3 cup cream or half & half
1/4 cup shredded or grated Parmesan or Romano cheese

Peel the squash, remove the seeds and cut the squash into small, about 1/2 inch square, cubes. Remove the casings from the sausage links and cut into slices about 1/2 inch thick. Set aside. Melt the butter in a skillet large enough to hold all the ingredients. Sauté the squash cubes until they begin to soften. Remove them from skillet and set aside. Put the sausage into the skillet and sauté until cooked and browned. If there is any grease in the skillet pour it off and discard. Return the squash to the skillet and cook the sausage and squash together for about 5 minutes on low heat. Add the cream and scrape up any crisp bits from the bottom of the skillet. Drain the pasta and toss together with squash, then sprinkle with cheese. Serve at once.

Pasta with Green Peas and Salmon

Serves 6

12 ounces linguini (or any other shape) cooked
8 to 12 ounces cooked fresh salmon
3 ounces butter
1 pound frozen green peas
1 teaspoon chopped or puréed garlic
juice and zest of 1 lemon

Melt the butter in a skillet large enough to hold all ingredients, a skillet attractive enough to go to the table is preferred. When butter is melted, stir in garlic and cook for about 1 minute then stir in peas and heat for a minute or two. Add pasta and salmon, cut in bite-size pieces, and toss to mix and heat salmon then stir in lemon juice and zest. Serve immediately.

Pad Thai

Serves 4

3 tablespoons vegetable oil
2 tablespoons chopped garlic
4 ounces rice noodles, about 1/4 inch wide
1 cake Pad Thai tofu (1/4 pound thinly sliced pork may be substituted)*
3 tablespoons chopped roasted peanuts
2 tablespoons salted turnip*
3 tablespoons dried shrimp*
1 cup fresh bean sprouts
1/2 cup Chinese chives or green onions, sliced 1 inch long
3 tablespoons fish sauce (nam pla)*
3 tablespoons lemon juice
2 eggs
1 lime, quartered
fresh coriander (cilantro) leaves

Place noodles in a bowl and pour boiling water over and leave to soak from 20 minutes to half an hour. The noodles must be quite soft. When soft, remove noodles from water and set aside. Slice the tofu into 1/8 inch layers and cut those into short julienne. Wash and cut chives or onion. Wash bean sprouts and set aside. Mix nam pla and lemon juice and set aside. Break eggs into small bowl and beat as for scrambled and set aside. Heat 2 tablespoons oil in wok and cook garlic until golden then add dried shrimp, turnip and bean curd or pork and continue to stir fry for a minute or so. Add noodles and fry for a minute or so to heat then add lemon juice and nam pla and toss to mix. Stir in half of bean sprouts, peanuts and chives or onion and stir fry for a minute or two. Push the noodle mixture aside up the side of the wok and add remaining oil and heat briefly. Then add egg and cook until it begins to set then stir noodle mixture into egg and cook, stirring gently, until egg is completely cooked. Turn Pad Thai onto platter and garnish with remaining peanuts, bean sprouts, chives, lime quarters and coriander leaves. Serve at once.

* Ingredients that can be obtained at most Oriental Markets.

Prik Nam Pla

4 tablespoons fish sauce
3 tablespoons lemon juice
1 small, fresh chilli pepper cut into rounds

Combine all ingredients and serve as a side dish with Thai dishes.

Fettucini with Fresh Tomato Sauce and Bacon

Serves 4 to 6
2 pounds fresh plum tomatoes
1 tablespoon butter
1 tablespoon chopped garlic
1/2 pound bacon
salt and pepper to taste
4 to 6 leaves fresh basil (optional)
1 pound fettucini, cooked and hot
1/2 cup grated Parmesan or Romano cheese

Cut tomatoes into cubes. Cut bacon slices into dice, fry crisply and drain. Pour off fat from skillet. Melt butter and cook garlic for about 2 minutes, do not brown, add tomatoes bring to simmer and season lightly with salt. After salting add basil if using. Add the drained, hot fettucini to the skillet and toss to thoroughly to coat with sauce. Remove to serving dish or if using a table-going skillet simply sprinkle bacon and cheese over and serve.

Vegetables

My Grandpa Lewis lived with us, my mother, father and me, and he was a skilled and enthusiastic gardener. The moment the ground was warm enough to start seeds, and in Mississippi that was early spring, he started the garden. There were spring onions, radishes and lettuces. Then came the English peas and new potatoes, and so it went until cold weather when the last few tomatoes ripened on the windowsill.

With this bounty there was always a variety of vegetables on the table. My mother canned hundreds of jars of vegetables and pickles for the winter. In addition, there were jams and jellies and canned fruits. My earliest introduction to this process, and I was an unwilling participant, was peeling literally washtubs of hot, cooked beets to make pickle. Exposure to all these wonderful vegetables started in me a life long love affair with them. I look forward as eagerly as did my grandfather to the arrival of the first seed catalog right after Christmas.

Quick Sweet and Sour Cabbage

Serves 4
1 jar (about 16 ounce) sweet and sour cabbage
1 medium size cooking apple, peeled and diced
1 small onion, peeled and diced
2 tablespoons vinegar
2 tablespoons either white or light brown sugar
pinch salt

Combine first five ingredients in a non-reactive pan (don't use aluminum) that can be used in the oven if desired. Cover tightly and cook for about 1/2 hour. If on top of stove use low heat, in oven 350°F. When mixture is hot and apple and onion are soft but not mushy taste for seasoning and add salt if desired.

Gourmet Alert! *Red Bliss potatoes are a delight, and with rosemary seasoning as in the next recipe they taste wonderful. They do take a little while, but you do have to cook the main course anyway!*

Sautéed Potatoes with Rosemary

Serves 4 to 6
about 2 pounds Red Bliss potatoes
2 tablespoons oil
2 tablespoons butter
salt and black pepper to taste
a few sprigs rosemary
chopped parsley if desired

Wash potatoes and cut into bite-size pieces but do not peel. Place in pan, cover with cold water and bring to boil. Turn down heat and simmer for about 15 minutes — only until easily pierced by knife but not soft. Remove from water and drain thoroughly. In skillet heat oil and add butter. When butter is starting to brown, add potatoes and rosemary and sauté until nicely browned. Drain on paper towels and salt and pepper to taste.

Note! *I gave the next recipe its name because of the layering of the ingredients, very like the layering in the famous dessert, "Napoleons."*

Eggplant 'Napoleons'

Serves 4 to 6
2 large eggplants
pan spray
1 pint ricotta cheese
1/4 cup torn basil leaves
1/2 cup or to taste grated Parmesan or Romano cheese
1/4 pound (approximately) Mozzarella cheese, grated
Fresh Tomato Sauce
Preheat oven to 350°F

Slice eggplant into rounds about 1/3 inch thick **DO NOT PEEL.** Spray a foil covered cookie sheet with pan spray and place eggplant slices on the foil and spray tops of slices. Place in oven until slices are lightly browned. **DO NOT TURN THEM.** Remove from oven. The eggplant can be cooked and refrigerated a day or two before using. It can also be used for other eggplant dishes, such as Eggplant Parmigiania.

Mix the ricotta with the basil and Parmesan or Romano cheese and, if you desire, add salt to taste. To cook the "Napoleons," cover a cookie sheet with foil or stay with the one you used to cook the slices. Lay 1/3 of the eggplant slices on the sheet. Place a heaping teaspoon of cheese mixture on eggplant and top with another slice, then more cheese. Top with the third and final slice and put a bit more cheese mix on top and finish with Mozzarella. Bake for about 30 minutes. Serve with a topping of Fresh Tomato Sauce. See recipe on page 103.

Note! *Sweet potatoes are a great treat, especially with pork dishes. Unfortunately they have been stereotyped as being very sweet combined with pineapple, sugar and marshmallows for holiday side dishes, and not really a vegetable. This is a pity because they are more interesting without all the added sweetness. Their natural, subtle sweetness blends so well with the gentle sweetness of most pork (or ham) dishes. Try this combination.*

Savory Sweet Potatoes

Serves 6 to 8
2 pounds, approximately, sweet potatoes
4 tablespoons butter, cut into bits
1/2 cup half & half or cream
1 teaspoon coarsely ground garlic powder
salt to taste and a good pinch cayenne pepper
Preheat oven to 400°F

Wash the potatoes and pierce in several places. Cook on foil lined baking pan in oven for about 1 hour or until they feel soft when squeezed. Remove from oven and allow to cool until they can be handled without burning your fingers. Remove and discard skins and mash pulp in butter. Stir in cream until potatoes are soft and fluffy but not soupy. Season to taste with salt then add garlic and cayenne. Place potatoes in an attractive, shallow oven proof gratin. Potatoes can be prepared to this point then covered and refrigerated. Bake at 350°F until hot and golden on top. Great with pork, poultry, or beefsteak.

Green Beans Parmigiana

Serves 4

1 pound green beans, fresh or frozen
3 tablespoons butter
1/2 cup shredded or grated Parmesan cheese

Cook beans until tender, if using frozen, follow packet directions. They may be cooked in advance and cooled in cold or ice water then drained thoroughly. Refrigerate if cooking in advance. When ready to prepare, heat butter in medium skillet and when sizzling, add beans and heat thoroughly. Immediately before serving, add cheese and toss to blend. Remove from heat and serve.

Curried Cabbage

Serves 4

1 small head cabbage, roughly chopped
2 heaping teaspoons Madras curry paste* (not powder)
1/2 cup half & half
salt to taste

Put the half & half and curry paste in a lidded pan, large enough to hold cabbage without crowding, stir to blend. Add cabbage, cover and cook on low heat for about 20 minutes, stirring occasionally, until cabbage is just tender. Watch closely, cabbage tends to burn. Season to taste.

* Available at Oriental markets, and many large supermarkets.

Butternut Squash Parmesan

Serves 4 to 6
1 1/2 pounds butternut squash
3 tablespoons butter
1/2 cup Parmesan cheese, grated

Cut squash in half lengthwise and remove seeds. Cook in microwave, cut side down, or bake in oven at 350°F, cut side down, until soft but not flabby. Scoop from skins, and discard the skins. Melt butter in small saucepan or skillet, add squash and mash with potato masher. Heat thoroughly and stir in cheese.

<u>Note</u>! *Well, here's a perennial favorite. You can control the "richness" of the mashed potatoes by controlling the amount of butter used in the mix. This recipe is "richer" than the mashed potato recipe given in the Cottage Pie in Beef Section.*

Mashed Potatoes

Serves 6
2 1/2 pounds, approximately, Red Bliss potatoes
1 stick butter
3/4 cup hot milk, approximately

Peel potatoes, if desired, and simmer until easily pierced with a knife, about 20 minutes. Mash or rice potatoes and then stir in the butter cut into small pieces. Stir in hot milk until potatoes are of desired consistency. Season with salt and pepper.

Note! *Mirleton, the other name is chayote, is a type of squash much loved in Louisiana, famous in song and story. It's about the size of an avocado but very pale green in color (about the color of iceberg lettuce) and is heavily wrinkled. It is the Shar Pei of the vegetable world.*

Mirleton Gratin

Serves 6
2 to 3 mirleton (chayotes)
1/2 pound ham (regular or country), finely chopped
5 ounce packet frozen, cooked shrimp
1 small onion, finely chopped
1 tablespoon parsley, finely chopped
1 teaspoon garlic, finely chopped
4 ounces (1 stick) butter
salt and pepper to taste
Preheat oven to 350°F

Boil the mirletons for about 15 to 20 minutes or until they can be easily pierced by a sharp knife. Sauté the vegetables and ham in the butter. Add the mirleton that has been seeded and cut into dice. There is no need to peel the mirletons. Sauté until all ingredients are soft and well blended, then season to taste. Thoroughly grease a gratin dish and put the mixture in and bake until browned, about 25 minutes.

Note! *The arrival of English peas and new potatoes signaled summer at our house. This is a very special side dish with a main course that isn't overly rich, such as roast chicken.*

Creamed Peas and New Potatoes

Serves 4 to 6
1 packet (1 pound) frozen green peas
1 pound baby potatoes, cooked
2 tablespoons butter
2 tablespoons flour
3/4 cup whole milk or half & half
salt and pepper to taste

Melt butter in 2-quart pan and add flour. Cook and stir over low heat for about 2 minutes then stir in milk being sure to eliminate all lumps. A whisk is helpful for this. Add peas to thaw and heat thoroughly add potatoes and be sure all is heated thoroughly. Salt and pepper to taste.

Note! *Cabbage, gently cooked, is a sweet and delicate vegetable. Cabbage has been the victim of overcooking and high heat cooking, giving it a reputation as bitter to the taste and evil to the nose. In fact, it's a tender baby, treat it lovingly and cook only until just tender.*

Braised Cabbage

Serves 4

about 1 1/2 pounds cabbage (1/2 medium head cabbage)
4 tablespoons butter
1/4 cup of half & half or cream
salt and pepper

Chop cabbage roughly, discarding core. Use a 2 to 3 quart pan or skillet with a lid. Melt butter, add cabbage and cover. Cook on medium heat, careful not to burn cabbage, stirring occasionally, for about ten minutes or until cabbage is wilted. Stir in cream. Salt and pepper lightly.

Pumpkin with Parmesan

Serves 4
1 can (approximately 1 pound) plain pumpkin
1/2 teaspoon salt, or to taste
1/4 teaspoon coarse garlic powder
1/2 cup shredded Parmesan cheese or 1/3 cup grated
1/4 cup half & half
1 egg, beaten
Preheat oven to 350°F

Mix all ingredients. Butter, or spray with pan spray, a glass pie dish or small gratin and fill with mixture. Bake until puffed and golden, about 30 minutes. Center should be 170°F. This is nice stuffed into miniature pumpkins and baked for about 1 hour to 1 1/2 hours.

Cooked Fresh Kale

Serves 4 to 6
1 to 1 1/2 pounds fresh kale
1/2 cup diced country ham or 2 tablespoons butter
1 cup water
salt to taste

Combine ham or butter with water in a pot with lid at least 3 1/2 quarts in volume. Bring water to a boil. Wash kale thoroughly and remove leafy parts from tough ribs and discard ribs. Place the kale in the boiling water, cover pot and turn heat to low and simmer until tender, about 20 minutes. Salt to taste.

Note! When you want sweet and sour cabbage it is so tempting to just "open a jar." To make the dish special, however you have to do something. Here is one answer!

Sweet and Sour Cabbage with Orange or Tangerine

Serves 4
1 jar purchased, sweet and sour cabbage
1 orange or tangerine

Empty the cabbage into a non-reactive (not aluminum or unclad iron) saucepan. Peel the orange or tangerine and if using orange, slice into rounds then quarters, and remove seeds. If using tangerine, divide into segments. Add the fruit to the cabbage and heat thoroughly. Serve with poultry or pork.

<u>Note</u>! We're back in the deep south again, where it's always time for grits. If you haven't tried it you're missing a treat. Not only is it a great medium for gravies and sauces of all kinds, but it can be flavored richly by the addition of some cheese, sausage, bacon, ham, and the list goes on. It's a blank canvas for the cook to develop a creation upon. There is nothing better for breakfast than country ham, fried eggs, grits and hot biscuits.

Grits

Serves 6
1 cup quick (not instant!) grits
4 cups water
1 teaspoon salt
3 tablespoons butter

In a 2-quart pot with lid, bring the water to a boil and add butter and salt. Pour in grits, stirring all the while. Turn heat to low and cover the pan. Cook for about 10 minutes, stirring occasionally to prevent sticking and lumping. If grits seem too thick add a bit more water; if too thin, cook for a few minutes with the lid off.

<u>Note!</u> You need an accompaniment for a curried dish? The recipe below is just what you want. It also goes well with many fish dishes.

Coconut Rice

Serves 4
1 cup converted rice
1 can (13.5 ounce) unsweetened coconut milk
1/4 cup (2 ounces) water
1/4 teaspoon salt or to taste
2 tablespoons butter
Preheat oven to 350°F

In a small, heavy pot with lid, melt the butter and when it sizzles, add the rice and cook, stirring occasionally until the rice grains begin to turn golden. Stir in the coconut milk and salt and use the water to swirl around the can to loosen the remaining coconut milk then add to the rice. Stir in the coconut, being sure to break up all lumps. Cook on low heat, tightly covered, for about 25 minutes, stirring occasionally to prevent sticking. Alternatively, bake, tightly covered in oven for about 35 minutes, stirring occasionally. This rice will be rather sticky because of the coconut.

Sautéed Red Bliss Potatoes with Almonds

Serves 4

1 1/2 to pounds Red Bliss potatoes
1/2 cup sliced almonds
4 tablespoons butter
salt and pepper

Wash potatoes and place in a pot and cover with cold water. Bring to a boil and turn down heat and simmer potatoes until they are still firm but can easily be pierced with a sharp knife. Cut in bite-size pieces. Melt butter in a medium-size skillet and allow butter to sizzle but don't brown. Place the potatoes in the pan being careful not to break them. Cook turning the pieces gently until they are golden brown then add almonds to the skillet and continue cooking until the almonds are golden. Salt and pepper to taste.

This is a perfect accompaniment for grilled salmon or tuna.

Green Beans Amandine

Serves 4
1 pound green beans, fresh or frozen
3 tablespoons butter
1/2 cup sliced almonds

Cook beans until tender, if using frozen, follow packet directions. They may be cooked in advance and cooled in cold or ice water then drained thoroughly. Refrigerate if cooking several hours in advance. When ready to prepare, heat butter in medium skillet and when sizzling, add beans and heat thoroughly. Immediately before serving, add almonds and toss to blend. Remove from heat and serve.

<u>Note</u>! *My grandpa was the type of gardener who believed in plenty with a capital P. Because of this bounty my Mama tried lots of recipes. This was one of my favorites.*

Southern "Fried" Corn

Serves 4
1 pound cut corn, fresh or frozen
3 tablespoons butter
salt to taste

Heat butter in skillet large enough to hold corn until butter sizzles briskly. Add corn and cook on medium high heat, stirring frequently, until it begins to brown. This takes about 15 minutes.

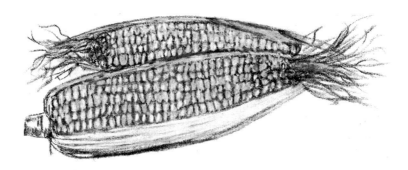

Sautéed Summer Squash with Onion

Serves 4
2 pounds yellow squash or patty pans (zucchini is too watery)
1 medium onion
3 tablespoons butter or bacon dripping
salt and pepper to taste

Dice the onion coarsely and slice the squash about 1/3 inch thick. Melt butter or dripping in medium skillet and when it is sizzling add the vegetables. Cook, turning frequently until most of the slices are well browned. Salt and pepper to taste.

Dressings and Sauces

Dressings make the salad, and sauces surely make the meal. Most of the art of cooking revolves around making good sauces and gravies. Almost any dish can be improved with a sauce and made great by a great sauce. In keeping with the premise of this book, there are some sauces presented that give quick results and are truly grand.

Note! *Dressings don't get any simpler than this, but it is a workhorse, and everyone needs to know it. Store leftover dressings in the refrigerator.*

Vinaigrette Dressing

3/4 cup extra virgin olive oil
1/4 cup wine or cider vinegar
salt and pepper to taste

Place all ingredients in jar with cover and shake well before using.

Note! *There are hundreds of variations on the simple Vinaigrette Dressing, and the one below is a great example*

Balsamic Vinaigrette Dressing

1/4 cup balsamic vinegar
1 cup extra virgin olive oil
salt and pepper to taste

Place all ingredients in jar with cover and shake well before using.

Note! *Here's another variation of the Vinaigrette Dressing.*

Green Peppercorn Salad Dressing

1 cup vegetable oil
1/3 cup wine vinegar
2 teaspoons salt
1 heaping tablespoon Dijon mustard
2 teaspoons brine packed green peppercorns, drained and crushed

Combine all ingredients and whisk vigorously until well blended. This dressing improves if allowed to blend, refrigerated for 24 hours.

Creamy Tomato Dressing

1 cup mayonnaise
1 medium tomato, puréed
2 tablespoons Crystal hot sauce
salt to taste

Purée tomatoes and mix thoroughly with the mayonnaise. Add Crystal and stir to mix. Season to taste.

__Note__! Here's a vegetable oil based Balsamic Vinegar Dressing.

Balsamic Dressing

1 cup vegetable oil
1/3 cup balsamic vinegar
1 tablespoon garlic purée
1 teaspoon salt

Combine all ingredients and whisk together until thoroughly blended. Refrigerate.

Dijon and Garlic Dressing

1 cup vegetable oil
1/4 cup cider or wine vinegar
1/2 cup Dijon mustard
2 tablespoons garlic purée
1 1/2 teaspoons salt

Combine all ingredients and process or beat until thoroughly emulsified. Refrigerate any unused portion.

Gourmet Alert! *This is an all time favorite. In recent years it has become dangerous because it has been made with raw eggs. Here's a great recipe that does not include raw eggs and still has the taste and feel of a true Caesar Dressing.*

Caesar Salad Dressing

1 teaspoon garlic purée
1 teaspoon Worcestershire sauce
1 teaspoon anchovy paste
juice of 1/2 lemon
1 teaspoon Dijon mustard
Pinch paprika
1 cup mayonnaise, preferably with no sugar
1/2 cup grated Parmesan or Romano cheese

Blend all ingredients in a food processor or mixer until well emulsified, about 2 minutes. The dressing will keep, well covered and refrigerated, for several weeks.

Mango Sauce

1 average size mango
1/4 cup Crystal hot sauce
juice of 2 medium limes
1/2 teaspoon salt or to taste

Peel, cut up and purée mango. It should give roughly 1 cup pulp. Add remaining ingredients and mix together thoroughly.

Gourmet Alert! *I have often thought that most people would happily eat door knobs, if they were in a sauce that's really tasty. Well this one is just that good.*

Marchand de Vin Sauce

4 ounces mushrooms, finely diced
1/2 cup country ham, finely diced
1/2 cup onion, finely diced
1/3 cup green onions, finely chopped
1 heaping tablespoon finely chopped or puréed garlic
6 tablespoons butter
4 tablespoons flour
3/4 cup, or as needed, chicken broth
3/4 cup dry red wine

In a heavy 8-inch saucepan or skillet, melt butter and sauté first 4 ingredients until tender but not browned. Stir in flour, stirring frequently, until browned, about 8 to 10 minutes. Add chicken broth and wine. Simmer, stirring occasionally, for a half hour or so or until thickened. The sauce should be nicely thickened but not heavy and solid. If needed add chicken broth until of a pleasant consistency. This sauce is delicious with chicken, eggs and beef.

Timesaver Alert! *The next few recipes are sure to become your favorites. They give you a way to make tomato sauces rapidly and with wonderful taste and body. No longer is it necessary to spend hours over a bubbling cauldron of tomatoes and a dozen other ingredients to prepare a dish with tomato sauce!*

Light Tomato Sauce

Serves 4 to 6
1 large can (1 pound, 12 ounce) chopped or crushed, unseasoned, tomatoes
2 heaping teaspoons, or to taste, basil pesto (commercial is fine)
salt and pepper to taste

Heat tomatoes to light simmer and then season lightly with salt. Add pesto to taste and pepper. This may be served, as is, on pasta or used to make Parmigiana. It may be used in any dish that requires tomato sauce.

Fresh Tomato Sauce

Serves 4 to 6
2 pounds fresh tomatoes
2 tablespoons butter or olive oil if preferred
salt and pepper to taste
fresh basil or pesto to taste

Skin tomatoes (method follows) and cut into vertical slices or cubes as desired. Melt butter in skillet and add tomatoes. Bring to simmer and season lightly with salt. After salting, add basil or pesto to taste. This sauce may be used in any dish that requires tomato sauce.

Note! *To Skin Tomatoes: Drop whole tomatoes into a pot of boiling water and remove in about 1 minute into a bowl of cold or ice water. As soon as they are cool enough to handle remove skins and use as desired.*

Quick Tomato Sauce

Serves 4-6
2 tablespoons extra virgin olive oil
salt to taste
and pinch dried thyme or 1/2 teaspoon fresh thyme leaves
1 teaspoon, or to taste, coarsely powdered garlic
1 can (28 ounce) crushed tomatoes

Heat tomatoes, and salt to taste and then add remaining ingredients.

Shallot And Tomato Sauce

Serves 4
3 to 4 shallots or 1 medium onion, diced
2 plum tomatoes, diced
1 tablespoon chopped garlic
3 or 4 sprigs coriander (cilantro), leaves only
2 tablespoons butter
1/4 cup white wine
1/4 cup heavy cream or sour cream
salt and pepper to taste

Over medium heat, melt butter in small skillet and sauté the onion until soft but not brown and add garlic and cook for 1 or 2 minutes. Add tomato and coriander and cook until totally wilted and juicy then add wine and cook for a few minutes until the sauce becomes thick and rather syrupy. Stir in cream and blend thoroughly and season to taste. This is delicious on sautéed pork or chicken cutlets.

Arrabbiata Sauce

1/4 cup virgin or extra virgin olive oil
2 tablespoons chopped garlic
1/2 teaspoon crushed red pepper
salt to taste
1 can (28 ounce) crushed tomatoes

Put oil, garlic, red pepper and 1/2 teaspoon salt in a heavy 2-quart pot or skillet and heat on low for 2 to 3 minutes or until garlic begins to turn golden, add tomato and allow to simmer for 15 minutes until sauce is well blended. Salt to taste.

Turkey Gravy

Serves 4-6

4 or more tablespoons pan drippings from the turkey roaster
equal amount by measure of flour
salt pepper and garlic to taste
broth
red wine if desired

In a medium-size saucepan heat the pan drippings and stir in flour to make a smooth paste. Cook and stir over medium heat until the mixture is a rich brown. Stir in turkey or chicken broth and wine (about two cups liquid) and whisk out any lumps. When the gravy begins to thicken more liquid will probably need to be added to achieve the desired consistency. Season to taste with salt and pepper and more garlic, if desired.

Fancied-up Cranberry Sauce

Serves 8 to 10

1 can (1 pound) whole berry cranberry sauce
1/4 cup orange marmalade

Combine above ingredients and serve.

Note! Another classic made easy!

Béchamel Sauce

2 cups whole milk or half & half
2 tablespoons butter
3 tablespoons flour
salt and pepper
nutmeg or garlic or cayenne or herbs to taste

Melt butter over low to moderate heat in a heavy saucepan, stir in flour and cook, stirring constantly, for about 2 minutes to eliminate the raw taste of the flour, but the butter must not be allowed to brown. Pour in the milk and bring to a gentle boil, whisking to incorporate the liquid and make a smooth, silky sauce. Lower heat to a simmer, whisking often, to reduce to the desired thickness. Season to taste with salt and desired seasoning. FOR A VELOUTÉ SAUCE FOR FISH OR CHICKEN SUBSTITUTE RICH CHICKEN BROTH FOR HALF THE MILK.

Note! This next sauce is named for the Duke of Cumberland who is hated and despised to this day in Scotland because of his brutality during and after the battle of Culloden, The sauce is good even if the duke wasn't.

Cumberland Sauce

2 tablespoon tangy jam or jelly (currant, plum or cranberry)
1 heaping teaspoon dry mustard
1 to 2 tablespoons port wine
zest and juice 1/2 orange
zest and juice 1/2 lemon
1/2 teaspoon salt

Melt jelly over low heat in small saucepan. Add remaining ingredients except port and simmer for 2 to 3 minutes add port and serve in sauceboat alongside poultry or pork.

Note*! No snails in this, just the seasoned butter in which they are traditionally cooked.*

Snail Butter

1 stick butter (4 ounce) at room temperature
1 large or 2 small cloves garlic, finely diced
2 shallots, finely diced
1/4 cup finely diced parsley

Combine all ingredients thoroughly and salt to taste.

Gourmet Alert! *You'll want to use this with many soups once you become familiar with it. Use just as much as you want plopped in the middle of the bowl of soup just before serving.*

Easy Rouille

1 cup mayonnaise (containing little or no sugar) do not use low fat
1 teaspoon finely minced garlic
a generous pinch paprika
salt to taste

Blend all ingredients together and refrigerate.

Country Gravy

3 tablespoons of vegetable oil or butter, or the oil that is in the skillet from "frying" whatever you will put the gravy on
3 tablespoons of flour
milk
garlic, finely chopped
salt and pepper to taste

Stir flour into the hot oil in skillet, and cook for about 2 minutes, stirring any crunchy bits in pan. Stir in enough milk to make a smooth gravy about the consistency of heavy cream. Stir in finely chopped garlic. Taste for seasonings, adding salt and pepper if necessary. Serve with cutlets of pork, beef or chicken or, mashed potatoes, white rice or biscuits.

Prik Nam Pla

4 tablespoons fish sauce
3 tablespoons lemon juice
1 chilli pepper cut into rounds

Combine all ingredients and serve as a side dish with Thai dishes.

Breads and Such

Bread has been called the staff of life. Every culture has had a bread or a bread-like dish that was special to it. Quick breads like biscuits and cornbread have been special to the south. Many Southerners never tasted yeast bread until the advent of packaged sliced bread. The introduction of self-rising flour in the early years of the 20th Century made for faster and easier biscuit making. Self-rising cornmeal came later and had the same effect on cornbread. Biscuits are perfect for any meal including tea. Cornbread is also delicious but once was considered to be déclassé for breakfast. For the record, biscuits are scones, but not all scones are biscuits.

Timesaver Alert! *Let's start with the best. These biscuits are so simple that truly anyone can make excellent biscuits with this recipe. Biscuits are so versatile, that they take equally well to being sandwiches with butter and Virginia ham for parties, or being partnered with gravy or eggs for breakfast.*

Buttermilk Biscuits

Makes 12 to 14 biscuits (about 2 inch diameter)
2 cups self-rising flour
1/4 cup solid vegetable shortening
1 cup (more or less) buttermilk
Preheat oven to 425°F

Line a baking pan or cookie sheet with foil and lightly oil. Cut shortening into flour with a table fork until the dough resembles cookie crumbs. Stir in buttermilk (the secret of good biscuits) about 1/3 at a time until the dough is well moistened but not soppy wet. Turn out onto lightly floured piece of wax paper and pat and knead gently into a ball and then flatten to about 1/4 to 1/2 inch thick (thinner biscuits are crisper and thicker have a softer crumb). Cut into rounds with 1-inch cutter for dainty biscuits, 2-inch for family size. Place biscuits into pan so that they are lightly touching. Bake 12 to 15 minutes or until golden brown.

Biscuits make a wonderful topping for chicken or meat pie, or fruit cobblers. They can also be split and buttered then filled and topped with strawberries and whipped cream for a delicious dessert.

Note! *This is a variation on the basic biscuit recipe above, but you won't believe how good this is with the black pepper. These are based on my friend, George Clark's biscuits. They have a real "bite".*

Black Pepper Biscuits

12 to 14 biscuits (about 2 inch diameter)
2 cups self-rising flour
1 tablespoon coarsely ground black pepper
1/4 cup shortening
3/4 cup (more or less) buttermilk
Preheat oven to 450° F

Lightly oil a baking pan or cookie sheet. Combine flour and pepper, and cut in shortening. Stir in buttermilk about 1/3 at a time until the dough is well moistened but not wet. Turn out onto lightly floured board and pat gently into a ball and then flatten to about 1/2 to 3/4 inch thick (thinner biscuits are crisper and thicker have a softer crumb). Cut into rounds with biscuit cutter. Bake 10 to 15 minutes or until golden brown.

Dumplings

2 cups self-rising flour
1 egg, beaten
3 tablespoons oil
2/3 cup milk or enough liquid to make a stiff dough

Bring about 4 quarts of water with 2 teaspoons salt to a boil in a pan with a lid. Combine egg, oil and 1/2 of the liquid and beat. Stir egg mixture into flour and mix, adding reserved liquid as needed. Drop dough in tablespoon-size balls into the boiling water. Reduce heat to simmer and cover pan. Cover and cook for about 12 minutes until dumplings float. Remove from water and serve with dishes that have gravy.

<u>**Gourmet Alert!**</u> *The following dumplings are very much like biscuit. The flour dusting on the dumplings thickens the broth and makes a rich gravy.*

Southern Dumplings

(for Chicken and Dumplings)
2 cups self-rising flour
1/3 cup soft shortening
1/2 cup milk

Work shortening into flour and add milk gradually to make a stiff dough. Sprinkle lightly with flour and roll out about 1/8 inch thick (a very thin sheet) and cut on the diagonal into diamonds. Dust lightly with flour and drop into boiling broth. Cover pot, lower heat and simmer for about 20 minutes. The dumplings are now ready to use in the stewed chicken. See recipe for Chicken and Dumplings in the Poultry Chapter.

Note! *The seasonings in this dressing are simmered in broth rather than cooking in butter; therefore it is less rich but extra flavorful.*

Basic Cornbread Dressing

Serves 8 to 10
8 cups crumbled cornbread
6 cups crumbled bread (see below)*
1 large onion, about 1 cup chopped
4 spears celery, diced
1 quart chicken or turkey broth
salt and black pepper to taste
3 tablespoons chopped parsley
3 tablespoons chopped fresh sage or 1 to 2 teaspoons dried or to taste
2 eggs

Simmer celery and onion in broth about 1/2 hour or until tender. Pour off broth to measure and add water to bring the amount back to 1 quart. Put broth, and cooked seasonings into large bowl. Crumble in corn bread.

*Put about 1 pound loaf of white bread (stale bread is best) in a separate bowl and cover with water. When bread is soaked, squeeze out water and measure bread. Add squeezed-out bread to broth, seasonings, cornbread mix and stir to mix. Salt and pepper and season with parsley and sage to taste. When seasoned to satisfaction, add eggs and stir in. Place in large greased baking pan and bake at 350° F for approximately 1 1/2 hours or until 190°F in center of pan.

To this basic dressing, before cooking could be added:
1 pound pork sausage, cooked and crumbled or
1/2 pound of roasted, peeled and chopped chestnuts or
1 pound sliced and sautéed mushrooms or
1 quart chopped oysters and liquid

Cornbread

makes enough for dressing above
3 cups self rising cornmeal
1 1/2 cups buttermilk
3 tablespoons vegetable oil
3 eggs
one 9-inch oven proof skillet, 2 tablespoons oil
preheat oven to 400°F

Swirl oil around skillet and heat until sizzling in oven or on top of stove. Combine all ingredients and place in hot skillet. Bake approximately 30 minutes or until done. This is a wonderful, light cornbread and can be made with the proportions of 1 cup meal, 1 egg, 1/2 cup buttermilk and 1 tablespoon oil.

Cheese Cornbread

Serves 4 to 6
2 cups self-rising corn meal
1/4 cup oil
2 large eggs
1 to 1 1/3 cups buttermilk
1 cup grated Cheddar or jalapeño cheese
a dash or two of pepper sauce
Preheat oven to 400°F

Heat a 10 to 12-inch oven proof pan, preferably cast iron and grease well. Combine corn meal, oil and eggs and add milk to make a rather soupy mix. Stir in cheese and pepper sauce. Bake for about 25 minutes or until done.

Cheese and Corn Cornbread

Serves 6
2 cups self-rising cornmeal
1 cup buttermilk
2 tablespoons vegetable oil
2 eggs
one 9-inch oven proof skillet
2 tablespoons oil
1 cup grated sharp Cheddar cheese
1 small can (about 8 ounces) whole corn kernels, drained
preheat oven to 400°F

Swirl oil around skillet and heat until sizzling in oven or on top of stove. Combine remaining ingredients and place in hot skillet. Bake approximately 30 minutes or until done.

Patty Cakes

Serves 4 to 6
2 cups corn meal (yellow stone ground preferred)
2 teaspoons salt
1 1/2–2 cups boiling water
2 or more as needed tablespoons oil

For a more interesting flavor, toast the corn meal in an ungreased pan at 350°F oven until it smells like popcorn. Combine, in a bowl, meal, salt and enough boiling water until the dough is just stuck together. Allow to cool until just warm to the touch. Using about 2 heaping tablespoons for each cake, flatten between palms of the hand to form a flat cake about 3 inches in diameter. Repeat until all dough is used. Sauté in oil at a level of about 1/2 depth of patty. Cook on both sides until golden brown. These should be cooked and eaten quickly because they do not retain their crispness.

Spaetzele

Serves 6
2 eggs
2 tablespoons vegetable oil or melted butter
1/2 cup water
1/2 cup milk
2 1/2 cups all purpose flour
1/2 teaspoon salt
1/2 teaspoon baking powder

Fill a large pot with water, 3 or 4 quarts, and add about 2 teaspoons salt to water. Bring to a boil. Mix all liquids, including eggs, and blend well. Combine dry ingredients and combine with liquids. The result will be quite stiff.

The spaetzele can be cooked by dropping dough by spoonfuls into the boiling water but this will be VERY slow. A spaetzele maker can be made as follows: Use a coffee can with holes cut in the bottom to hold the raw dough and to press out "Strings" of spaetzele into the boiling water. The holes can be conveniently made in the bottom of the coffee can with a "church key" (one of those old beer can openers that has a triangular knife-like device at the end that you use to puncture tinned milk and other cans of liquid. The dough can be pushed through the holes in the bottom of the can with a soft spatula or a potato masher that has been covered with foil. Spaetzele will float when done, about 5 minutes.

Polenta

Serves 6
5 cups water
1 pound stone ground yellow corn meal
salt to taste

Bring the water to boil and reduce heat. Whisk in corn meal continue to whisk out lumps. Reduce heat to very low and continue cooking, stirring frequently, for about 20 minutes. Season to taste with salt. Pour onto cookie sheet to cool. If eaten hot, season liberally with lightly sautéed diced garlic, butter and cheese. If chilled, cut into squares and overlap in baking dish, sprinkle with grated cheese of your choice and baked at 350°F until cheese is bubbly and polenta is hot. This is a good accompaniment to most meat and fish dishes.

<u>**Gourmet Alert!**</u> *Breadmaking doesn't get any easier than this. Using self-rising flour is not traditional but the result is wonderful.*

Irish Soda Bread

Serves 4 to 6
2 cups self-rising flour
1 cup buttermilk
Preheat oven to 350°F

Stir milk and flour together to make a stiff (not sticky) dough. Knead gently and work dough into a ball. Flatten slightly and transfer to foil-lined pan, sprayed with pan spray. Cut a cross into top of ball and brush with melted butter, or cream or spray heavily with pan spray. Bake 45 minutes to an hour. Bread should be golden and sound hollow when rapped with the knuckles.

Irish Soda Bread with Cheese and Walnuts

Serves 6
2 cups self-rising flour
1 cup buttermilk
6 ounces grated sharp Cheddar cheese
1 cup broken walnuts
Preheat oven to 350°F

Stir flour and milk together to make a stiff (not sticky) dough. Knead gently and work in half the cheese and all the walnuts and form dough into a ball. Flatten slightly and transfer to foil-lined pan, sprayed with pan spray. Sprinkle remaining cheese over the dough. Cut a cross into top of ball. Bake for 45 minutes to an hour. The bread should be golden and sound hollow when rapped with the knuckles and the bread should be crusty and golden with the cheese.

Desserts

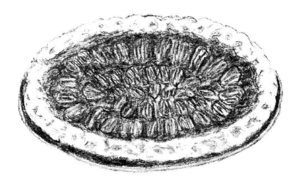

Hospitality was and is a way of life among Southerners. A visitor would barely be inside the front gate before my mama was asking what they would like to drink. No matter the season the drinks were always the same: hot coffee, iced tea and cold Coke. If the guest was willing to "sit a spell", the next question would be "How about a piece of cake," or pie or whatever was available. Of course, there was always something sweet to be had, as there would have been in most southern homes. Southerners are known for having a sweet-tooth and the women were famous for their light hands with cakes and pies.

Most of the desserts here are so easy that even the busiest person can whip up something special for their family, or for a friend who drops in.

Note! *This is a very pretty creation, red and blue with drifts of white. Why not make this patriotically colored dessert for the Fourth of July?*

All American Dessert

1 pint heavy whipping cream
3/4 cup granulated sugar
1 teaspoon vanilla
1 pint blueberries
1 pint strawberries

Whip cream with sugar and vanilla until very stiff. Rinse berries and drain on paper towels until they are dry. Remove caps and slice strawberries, reserving 2 or 3 strawberries and a few blueberries for garnish. Gently fold berries into cream. Serve in an attractive bowl, and garnish with reserved berries. Serve immediately.

Strawberry Fool

Serves 4
1 pint thoroughly ripe strawberries
1/3 cup sugar or to taste
1/2 pint whipping cream, whipped
1/2 cup vanilla cookie crumbs

Mash strawberries with potato masher and sweeten to taste, stir in cookie crumbs and fold in whipped cream. Serve at once or place in freezer until lightly frozen. Recipe may be doubled.

Gourmet Alert! *My daddy made the ambrosia for holidays, Thanksgiving and Christmas. The oranges' pulp was carefully separated from the pith and seeds, and set aside. Grating coconut was a ritual; first, the draining of the water when the "eyes" were pierced, then the shells and brown skin were removed so the snow white meat was available to be shredded. The fruit needed only a touch of powdered sugar to finish. This recipe is much easier but the results are very much the same.*

Southern Ambrosia

Serves 8 to 10

1 bag (5 pound) oranges, peeled, pith and seeds removed
2 packages (1 pound each) sweetened grated coconut

Make alternate layers of coconut and orange pulp, beginning and ending with coconut. This is best made the day before and allowed to rest in the refrigerator overnight before using.

Banana and Toffee Fool

Serves 4
1/2 pint heavy whipping cream
2 medium to large bananas, sliced
1/2 cup crushed Heath bars
2 tablespoons granulated sugar
1 teaspoon vanilla

Whip cream to soft peaks, add sugar and vanilla then resume beating and whip stiffly. Fold sliced bananas and toffee into cream and chill for at least 30 minutes before serving.

Strawberries with Ricotta

Serves 4
1 pint fresh strawberries
1 1/2 cups ricotta
1 tablespoon balsamic vinegar, optional
1 cup sugar
dash cinnamon

Wash and stem strawberries and slice into serving dish. If berries are very flavorful sweeten with 1/2 cup of sugar and balsamic vinegar is optional. If berries have little flavor the vinegar will brighten the flavor. Set the berries aside to steep. Stir the remaining 1/2 cup sugar into the ricotta and add a dash or two of cinnamon. Stir to blend. Serve the ricotta mixture over the strawberries

Whipped Cream

Serves 4
1/2 pint heavy whipping cream
1/4 cup granulated sugar
1/2 teaspoon vanilla

Beat cream until it begins to thicken then add sugar gradually. Beat in vanilla. Beat until cream is very thick but don't over beat or it will turn into butter.

Note! *I use brown sugar for sweetness and flavor. When I want sweetness only, I use granulated sugar.*

Dessert, Quick and Easy

Serves 4
1 can (approximately 1 pound) sliced or diced pineapple
2 oranges, peeled and sliced across grain
1/4 cup light brown sugar, packed
1/2 teaspoon cinnamon

Combine all ingredients and serve cold or hot. Can be served over waffles or pound cake, or on its own.

Gourmet Alert! *The dressing that accompanies the compote below tastes good enough to drink. The dressing can be used with many fruit combinations for a world of different compotes. Don't use it with whipped cream because the flavors will fight.*

Orange Compote

Serves 6
6 oranges peeled and sliced

Fruit Salad Dressing

2 cups white wine
1 cup granulated sugar
a pinch of cayenne pepper
1/4 teaspoon cinnamon
juice of 1/2 lemon
a pinch of salt

Bring wine and sugar to a gentle boil and simmer for about 3 minutes. Add spices and salt and simmer for another 2 minutes. Remove from heat and stir in lemon juice. Pour over oranges and chill before serving. The dressing will keep almost indefinitely in refrigerator, if well sealed. It's good on any mix of fresh fruit salad.

Fruit Salad

Serves 4 to 6
1 medium pineapple, peeled, cored and cut into bites
1 pint strawberries, washed, capped and cut
2 firm-ripe bananas
1/2 cup light brown sugar, packed
1/2 teaspoon cinnamon

Just before dinner, combine all ingredients and leave at room temperature until dessert time. If made too far ahead the bananas will turn brown.

Blushing Fruit Salad

Serves 6
1 medium cantaloupe
2 large oranges
1 cup raspberries, fresh or frozen
1/2 cup granulated sugar

Wash cantaloupe, peel and seed and cut into bites. Wash and peel oranges and slice into circles across the segments and quarter circles. Purée the raspberries and sugar and toss with the fruit.

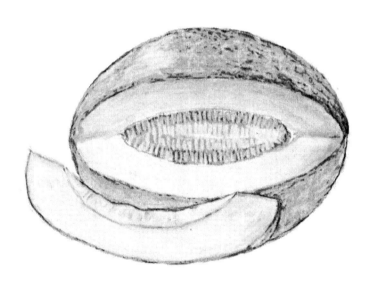

Summertime Dessert

Serves 4
1 pint strawberries
1 lemon
1/2 cup sugar
2 small cantaloupes

Wash cantaloupes, cut in halves and remove seeds. Place each on a dessert dish. (Cut a small slice from the bottom of the melon half so it will sit upright on the plate.) Rinse and cap strawberries and cut into quarters. Sprinkle berries with the juice of the lemon and sprinkle with the sugar and toss lightly to blend. Divide the berries among the cantaloupe halves. Serve at once.

A Compote Of Strawberries And Apricots

1 pint strawberries, as red as possible
1 pound fresh, ripe apricots
1/4 cup granulated sugar
1/2 cup orange juice
1/4 cup orange liqueur

Wash apricots but do not peel. Cut the apricots in half and remove seeds then cut each half in half. Cut the strawberries in halves or quarters depending upon the size of the berries. Pieces should be cut to the size of the apricot pieces. Combine fruit and place in an attractive glass bowl. Combine the juice, liqueur and sugar and stir to dissolve sugar. Toss liquid with fruit about 10 minutes before serving. The fruit should be at room temperature or only slightly cooler, not refrigerator cold. When the fruit is too cold the flavors are dulled.

Note! *"Crisps" and "grunts" are old-fashioned fruit desserts. They have stood the test of time because they are so good.*

Apple Crisp

Serves 4 to 6
2 pounds apples, peeled and sliced (about 5 cups) or
1 can (20 ounce) unsweetened sliced apples may be used
1/4 cup water
1 cup light brown sugar, firmly packed
1 teaspoon cinnamon
pinch salt
3/4 cup all-purpose flour
1 stick butter
Preheat oven to 350°F

Put apples in shallow 2-quart baking dish and add water. Combine all dry ingredients in a bowl and cut in butter. Sprinkle over apples and cover with foil. Bake for 30 minutes. Uncover and bake for 30 minutes more.

If using canned apples, sprinkle butter mixture over apples. Bake uncovered for 30 minutes or until medium gold in color.

Note! *Fried apples are very good for breakfast with biscuits or pancakes and ham, sausage or bacon. Think of this combination when the family is shoveling snow and appetites are lusty.*

Fried Apples

Serves 4 to 6
4 large cooking apples (Granny Smith for example)
1 tablespoon vegetable oil
3 tablespoons butter
salt to taste
2 tablespoons light brown sugar, packed

Quarter and core apples and if peelings aren't tough don't peel. Slice from top to bottom in about 1/4 inch slices. Melt butter in oil in skillet and when sizzling add apples and cook over moderate heat, turning often. Cook about 15 minutes or until lightly browned and tender but not mushy. Salt to taste, and sprinkle with sugar.

Apple Sauce

Serves 4
2 pounds tart apples
granulated sugar to taste

Quarter and core but don't peel apples. Place in pan with just enough water to keep apples from sticking. Cover pan, cook on low medium heat for about 30 minutes or until soft. Push through colander to remove solids.

Profiteroles
(Cream Puffs)

Serves 6 to 8
3/4 cup water
1/4 cup milk
1/4 teaspoon salt
1 stick butter
1 1/4 cups sifted all-purpose flour
4 eggs
Preheat oven to 375°F

Place water, milk and salt in saucepan and bring almost to a boil and add butter. Bring to a boil and add flour all at once, turn down heat and cook and stir for about 2 minutes mashing the dough down and stirring together until the dough comes together and forms a ball in the pan. Remove from heat and allow to cool until the dough is comfortable to the touch (if it is too hot it will cook the eggs). In the pan or a metal bowl, beat the eggs into the dough with an electric mixer, one at a time, until the dough is smooth and silky and stands in gentle peaks. Form shapes 1 inch in diameter, remembering that the dough swells to about 3 times its raw size when baked. Bake on foil-lined baking sheet, which has been sprayed lightly with pan spray until a rich chestnut brown. When cool, slice open and fill with ice cream or whipped cream and top with Chocolate Fondue Sauce, in this Chapter. These are always served in threes.

Georgia Peach Cobbler

Serves 6
1 stick butter
3/4 cup self-rising flour
1 cup granulated sugar
1/2 cup light brown sugar, packed
1 teaspoon vanilla
1/2 teaspoon cinnamon
3/4 cup milk
2 cups peeled, sliced fresh peaches (about 2 pounds) or
1 package (16 ounce) unsweetened frozen peaches
Preheat oven to 350°F

Spray an 8-inch square or equivalent size pan with pan spray. Place peaches in pan and chop butter in small bits over top. Sprinkle brown sugar and cinnamon over fruit. In separate bowl, stir vanilla into milk and add to a mix of the flour and granulated sugar. Stir together well. Spoon batter over fruit and smooth over top. Bake for about 1 hour, until topping is browned and well risen.

Apple and Prune Clafouti

Serves 6
4 large eggs
1 1/2 cups milk
1/2 cup plus 2 tablespoons granulated sugar
1/2 teaspoon cinnamon
1 teaspoon vanilla
pinch salt
3/4 cup all-purpose flour
1/2 cup moist, pitted prunes
2 apples, peeled and thinly sliced
1/2 stick butter
Preheat oven to 375°F

Heat milk with butter until butter is melted. Remove from heat. Whisk eggs with 1/2 cup sugar, cinnamon and vanilla. Add to milk-butter mix and finally add flour and salt. Whisk until there are no lumps. Butter or spray well with pan spray a 9-inch round baking pan (about 1 3/4 inches deep) and distribute apple slices and prunes around bottom. Pour batter over and gently smooth top. Bake for about 1 1/2 hours. Midway through cooking time, sprinkle the remaining 2 tablespoons sugar over top. Bake until the top is richly golden and puffed. Allow to cool long enough that the clafouti can be handled. Loosen from pan with spatula and slide out the whole clafouti onto serving dish. Serve with ice cream, custard or whipped cream.

Blueberry Peach Crumble

Serves 6

Filling

2 cups blueberries (fresh or frozen)
1 cup (about 4 ounces) peach slices (fresh or frozen)
1/2 cup granulated sugar
dusting of cinnamon
juice of 1/2 lemon

Grease with butter or spray with pan spray a baking dish, approximately 8 inchs x 8 inchs x 2 inchs, glass for preference (it won't stain). Place fruit in baking dish and sprinkle with remaining ingredients.

Topping

1 stick cold butter
3/4 cup light brown sugar, packed
3/4 cup quick oatmeal (not instant)
3/4 cup all-purpose flour
Preheat oven to 375°F

Cut butter into remaining ingredients by hand or with a food processor until well blended but not greasy. Sprinkle over fruit filling and bake for about 30 minutes until top is well browned and fruit bubbly.

This is really special with vanilla ice cream.

Sticky Biscuits

Serves 6 to 8
2 cups plus 1/2 cup self-rising flour
1/4 cup shortening
1 cup, approximately, buttermilk
1/2 stick butter
1/2 cup sugar cane syrup
1 cup pecans
Preheat oven to 375°F

Stir shortening into 2 cups of the flour and add milk to make a moist but not sticky dough. Put 1/2 cup of flour on piece of waxed paper and scrape dough out of bowl onto paper. Knead gently until dough is smooth. Melt butter and stir in syrup well. Pat dough to a thickness roughly 1/2 inch and cut in rounds about 2 inches in diameter. Pour 1/2 of butter-syrup mix into 9-inch diameter pan and spread pecans over. Place biscuit rounds over pecans and pour remaining syrup butter mix over. Bake for about 20 minutes, or until nicely browned on top and biscuits are baked through. Let rest for about 5 minutes then place plate over top and invert CAREFULLY. Scrape any remaining syrup out and spread over top.

Gourmet Alert! This next dessert is a particular favorite of mine. It works well for brunch. It fairly cries out for a cup of coffee.

Apple-Cheese Cobbler

Serves 6 to 8
2 cups self-rising flour
1/3 cup butter, at room temperature
1 cup, approximately, buttermilk
5 ounces sharp Cheddar cheese, grated
2 cans (20 ounce each) unsweetened sliced apples
1/2 cup (packed) light brown sugar
dash cinnamon
Preheat oven to 400°F

Combine apples, sugar and cinnamon and spread in bottom of a 2 to 3-pint ovenproof baking dish. In a separate bowl, mash butter into flour and moisten well with buttermilk. The mixture should be wet but not sloppy. Stir in about 4 ounces of cheese. With two tablespoons make balls about the size of a plum and ring the baking dish on top of the apples, then make additional balls for the center. If you have too much dough just make a couple of biscuits to bake beside the cobbler. Sprinkle the remaining cheese on top of the cobbles. Place the baking dish inside a foil-lined baking pan to prevent spills. Bake 20 to 30 minutes until nicely browned and cobbles are done on bottom. (It's all right to peek.) Allow to cool for a few minutes before serving.

Mango Clafouti

Serves 6

4 large eggs
1 1/2 cups milk
1/2 stick butter
1/2 cup plus 2 tablespoons granulated sugar
1/2 teaspoon cinnamon
1 teaspoon vanilla
pinch salt
3/4 cup all-purpose flour
2 mangoes, peeled and chopped
Preheat oven to 375°F

Heat milk with butter until butter is melted. Remove from heat. In separate bowl, whisk eggs with 1/2 cup sugar, cinnamon and vanilla. Add to milk-butter mix and finally add flour and salt. Whisk until there are no lumps. Spray well, a round 9-inch baking pan about 1 3/4 inches deep, with pan spray. Distribute mango pieces in the bottom of the pan, and pour batter over, gently smoothing top. Bake for about 1 1/2 hours. Midway through cooking time sprinkle the remaining 2 tablespoons of sugar over top. Bake until the top is richly golden and top is puffed. Allow to cool long enough that the clafouti can be handled. Loosen from pan with spatula and slide out whole onto serving dish.

Blueberry Bread

Serves 6 to 8
3 cups self-rising flour, reserve 3 tablespoons to toss with berries
1/2 cup granulated sugar
1/2 cup light brown sugar, packed
2 large eggs
1 cup buttermilk
1/3 cup vegetable oil
1 pint blueberries
Preheat oven to 350°F

Rinse and drain berries and then allow to drain on paper towels. Beat eggs and sugars and beat in milk and oil. Add flour and stir only until flour is moistened. With reserved flour, dust berries and fold in gently. Bake in a well-oiled loaf or 9-inch cake pan until done. This will take 35 minutes to an hour depending on the pan. Insert a toothpick in center and if done it will come out clean.

Brownie Cobbler

Serves 6 to 8
8 ounces raspberries, fresh or unsweetened frozen
3/4 cup granulated sugar
6 ounces semi-sweet chocolate bits, 1 cup
5 1/3 tablespoons butter
2 large eggs
1/2 cup granulated sugar
1/2 cup all-purpose flour
1/2 teaspoon baking powder
1 teaspoon vanilla
1 cup broken walnuts
Preheat oven to 350°F

Spray a "brownie pan" or an 8 or 9-inch round pan with pan spray. Spread raspberries evenly in bottom of pan and sprinkle 3/4 cup of sugar over.

Melt chocolate bits and butter over hot water or in microwave. In a separate metal bowl, beat the eggs with the 1/2 cup sugar until very thick and lemon colored. Lightly beat in the flour, baking powder, chocolate and butter mixture and the vanilla. Spread gently over the raspberries. Bake for about 25 minutes. A knife or toothpick stuck into the center should come out clean. Serve warm or cold. Warm with ice cream, Brownie Cobbler is special.

Blueberry Muffins

Serves 6 to 8
2 2/3 cups self-rising flour, set aside about 2 tablespoons of flour to toss with blueberries
1/2 cup sugar
1 cup buttermilk
2 large eggs
1/2 cup vegetable oil
1 1/2 cups blueberries, rinsed
Preheat oven to 375°F

Drain blueberries on paper towels. When dry, pour berries into a dish and toss with 2 tablespoons flour. Combine remaining flour and sugar. Stir in liquid ingredients and stir in only until dry ingredients are moistened. Gently fold in the floured blueberries. Line muffin cups with foil or paper liners or spray muffin cups with pan spray and fill them 2/3 full. Bake for about 25 minutes. A toothpick, inserted in center will come out clean.

Blueberry and Apple Charlotte

Serves 4 to 6
1 pint blueberries, picked over, washed and drained
1 can (20 ounce) plain canned apples,
1 cup granulated sugar
8 ounces good white bread, crusts removed and bread cubed
1 stick butter, melted
1 teaspoon cinnamon
juice of 2 lemons
Preheat oven to 375°F

Combine all ingredients and turn into a 2 1/2 to 3-pint oven proof baking dish, buttered or oiled. Place the baking dish inside a foil-lined baking pan to prevent spills. . Bake 30 to 35 minutes until nicely browned . Allow to cool for a few minutes before serving.

Plum and Apple Cobbler

Serves 6 to 8

1 can (30 ounce) of whole plums, drained (save juice)
1 can (20 ounce) unsweetened apples, drained, discard juice
1 cup granulated sugar
1/2 teaspoon almond extract
2 cups self-rising flour
1/3 cup shortening
1 cup buttermilk, approximately
1 ounce sliced almonds
2 tablespoons granulated sugar
Preheat oven to 375°F

Cut plums in half and remove stones. Combine plums and apples, in 2 1/2 to 3-pint ovenproof baking dish, buttered or oiled. Dissolve sugar in 1/2 cup plum juice and add almond extract. Pour over fruit, add more juice, if necessary, to bring juice level almost to top of fruit. In separate bowl, stir shortening into flour and moisten well with buttermilk. The mixture should be wet but not sloppy. With two tablespoons make balls about the size of a plum and place them in a ring around the edge of the baking dish on top of the fruit. Then make additional balls for the center. If you have too much dough just make a couple of biscuits to bake beside the cobbler. Sprinkle the almonds and sugar top of the cobbles. Place the baking dish inside a foil-lined baking pan to prevent spills. Bake 30 to 35 minutes until nicely browned and cobbles are done on bottom. Its all right to peek. Allow to cool for a few minutes before serving. Great with cream or ice cream.

Blonde Mincemeat

Enough for 2 pies
4 ounces each candied orange and lemon peel
1 pound dried apricots
1 cup golden raisins
1 can (20 ounce) crushed pineapple
1 1/2 cups granulated sugar
1 cup white rum
1 slightly rounded teaspoon cinnamon
grated juice and zest of 1 orange

Grind coarsely the first 3 ingredients in food processor. Combine all ingredients and simmer for about 10 minutes stirring constantly – it burns easily. Keeps well refrigerated.

Praline Bananas

Serves 6
3 large, firm bananas, peeled and sliced in half lengthwise
1 stick butter
1 cup light brown sugar, firmly packed
1/2 cup pecans
1/2 cup heavy cream

In a large, heavy skillet, melt the butter and when sizzling, sauté the bananas until golden, turn and brown the other side. Remove the bananas from the skillet and stir in the brown sugar. Stir the sugar and butter until the sugar is melted then add the cream, a bit at the time, stirring until the mixture "comes together." Return bananas to the pan. Serve over waffles, pancakes or ice cream.

<u>*Note*</u>*! Plantains are the big brothers of the banana family. They are always served cooked. When green they are sliced thinly and fried to make chips or served cooked as side dishes. Plantains sweeten slightly as they ripen. They are allowed to ripen completely for use in desserts. They have always been available in New Orleans but are newcomers elsewhere.*

Plantains for Dessert

1/2 very ripe plantain per person
butter
powdered sugar

Choose plantains that are completely black or are heavily mottled black with little yellow showing. Rinse the plantains and with a knife, cut the ends off them. Slice the fruit in half, cutting through the equator. Peel the fruit by cutting the peelings away. Cut the plantains lengthwise into slices about 1/4 inch thick. Sauté the slices in butter until they are a medium brown and feel tender when pierced with a knife. Remove from skillet and sprinkle with powdered sugar.

Baked Apples with Blackberry Jam

Serves 6
6 medium size Golden Delicious apples
blackberry jam
cinnamon
table cream or ice cream
Preheat oven to 350°F

Core the apples about two-thirds of the way through, being careful not to pierce the bottom and peel them about one half the way down the fruit. Put a tablespoon of jam in the cored hole and sprinkle the top with just a whisper of cinnamon. Place apples in a baking dish with about an inch water in bottom of dish, just enough to keep them from sticking, and bake for about 30 minutes or until apples are just tender but not mushy. Serve with cream or ice cream if desired.

Peach and Pineapple Cobbler

Serves 8 to 10
1 1/2 pound bag frozen unsweetened peaches
1 medium-size pineapple
1 teaspoon cinnamon
1 cup light brown sugar, packed
Topping
3 cups self-rising flour
1/2 teaspoon cinnamon
1/2 cup, packed, light brown sugar
1 1/2 cups buttermilk
1/2 cup shortening
Preheat oven to 375°F

Allow peaches to thaw. Wash, peel and dice pineapple. Combine fruits with cinnamon and sugar and stir to mix. Pour fruit mixture into a buttered or oiled 10-inch round pan, 2 to 3 inches deep, and smooth to level fruit. Prepare topping by combining dry ingredients in a bowl then stirring in the shortening and the buttermilk to make a wet but not soupy dough. Cover the top of the fruit mixture with spoonfuls of dough and place the baking pan or dish on a foil lined cookie sheet. Bake for about 30 minutes, then reduce heat to 350°F and bake until top is well browned and the filling is bubbly. Cooking will take from an hour to an hour and a half, depending on the temperature of and the amount of fruit. Check the doneness of the topping by gently lifting one of the dough mounds, the bottom should not look wet and raw. If it does, cook a bit longer and check again. The dough should look cooked.

Banana Gingerbread

Serves 8

2 large, but not huge, ripe bananas
2 cups plus 2 tablespoons self-rising flour
1/2 teaspoon bicarbonate of soda (baking soda)
1 tablespoon cinnamon
1 tablespoon ground ginger
1/2 cup, packed, light brown sugar
2 large eggs
4 tablespoons cane syrup or light molasses
2 tablespoons vegetable oil
3 ounces orange juice
Preheat oven to 325°F

Combine dry ingredients and sugar in a metal or plastic mixing bowl. In another dish mash the bananas and to them add the eggs, syrup, oil and orange juice and combine well. Add the banana mixture to the dry ingredients and beat to mix thoroughly. Pour into a greased and waxpaper-lined 9-inch square or round pan. Bake for about 45 minutes and cool in the pan. When cool, wrap in foil or plastic and set aside until the next day. The flavors must blend.

Chocolate Fondue

Serves 6 to 8
12 ounces semi-sweet chocolate bits
1 1/4 cups whipping cream or evaporated whole milk
1/4 cup white corn syrup

Melt chocolate in the cream, gently, over low heat. Refrigerate between uses. It is wonderful for dipping fruit or served warm, as a sauce over ice cream or profiteroles. Keeps well in refrigerator.

Special Peach Pie

Serves 6
1 sheet purchased puff pastry dough
12 ounces frozen sliced peaches
or 2 pounds fresh peaches, sliced
3/4 cup granulated sugar
2 tablespoons butter
a pinch cayenne pepper
1/2 teaspoon cinnamon
juice of 1/2 lemon
1 pint heavy whipping cream
1 tablespoon Bourbon whiskey
1/3 cup light brown sugar, packed
Preheat oven to 400°F

You will need two 9-inch pie pans, glass is preferred, because you can see how things are progressing, but metal will do nicely. Thaw puff pastry sheet and unfold. On a sheet of waxed paper spread a light film of flour. Roll the pastry so that it is wide enough to fit into the pie tin and allow overhang. Crimp the dough around the rim of the pan and tuck it slightly under the edges to discourage the dough from pulling away from the sides. Place the dough-lined pan in the oven for about 3 minutes to firm the surface.

Remove from oven and set the other pan on the dough. If using glass it is heavy enough but if using metal weigh with a glass or bottle that will withstand the oven temperature. Return to oven. When the edges begin to turn golden, remove the covering pie pan to brown the center of the shell. If the dough starts to puff, push it down and when it is removed from oven prick a tiny air hole in center and gently squish the air out. Allow to cool.

Melt the butter in a pan large enough to hold peaches and pour in peaches and sugar. Heat the peaches until they start to give off juice then remove the peaches from the juice into a bowl. Bring the juice to a boil and reduce to the thickness of syrup. Add the cayenne and cinnamon and stir. Remove from heat and add lemon juice. Pour over peaches and allow to cool.

Beat cream with brown sugar and Bourbon until quite stiff.

Just before serving put peaches in the pie crust and top with whipped cream. Refrigerate leftovers.

<u>Gourmet Alert!</u> *This next recipe is an absolutely delicious lemon pie. It is pleasantly tart and has a very nice texture. Squeezing the lemons is the most time consuming step in the preparation.*

Luscious Lemon Pie

Serves 6 to 8

2/3 cup, fresh lemon juice (fresh juice is essential) this will be 4 to 6 lemons, depending on size grated zest from 1 lemon (zest before cutting and squeezing, it's easier)
3 tablespoons sour cream
5 large eggs
9-inch pie shell (purchased frozen will do nicely)
1 cup granulated sugar
Preheat oven to 350°F

Bake pie shell until lightly golden (about 10 minutes) and cool before adding remainder of ingredients. In a large bowl whisk together the lemon juice, zest, sour cream and sugar until well blended and the sugar is dissolved. Beat in eggs, one at a time, beating thoroughly after each addition. Pour into pie shell that has been placed on a foil-lined baking pan, to prevent spills. Bake for about 30 minutes until lightly golden and firm. If in doubt about doneness, check temperature of pie with an "instant read" kitchen thermometer*. The temperature in middle of filling in the center of the pie should be 170°F. At that temperature the eggs will be safe to eat. Cool before serving. This is very good served with a dollop of sour cream or a scoop of vanilla ice cream.

* Instant read cooking thermometers are available in the gadget section of most supermarkets.

French Pear Pie

Serves 6
3 ripe pears
3 large eggs
1/2 cup granulated sugar
1 teaspoon vanilla
zest and juice of 1 lemon
1 cup sour cream
1-9 inch deep pie shell
Preheat oven to 350°F

Peel, halve and core pears. Place each half into pie shell core side down and small end toward center. You probably will only need 21/2 pears unless they are unusually narrow. In a medium bowl mix all remaining ingredients. Place pie pan on foil-covered cookie sheet to protect oven because the pie shell will be very full. Pour the mixture over the pears and place in oven and bake for approximately 1 hour until lightly golden around edges and puffed in center. The temperature in the center should be 170°F.

Marlboro Pie

Serves 6 to 8
9 inch deep dish pie shell prebaked until starting to firm but not brown
1 lemon, juice and grated rind
1 cup light brown sugar, packed
1 tablespoon all-purpose flour
pinch salt
4 large eggs
2 cups unsweetened applesauce (purchased or homemade)
1 teaspoon vanilla
3 tablespoons butter, melted
Preheat oven to 350°F

Wash lemon, grate rind and squeeze juice. Blend sugar, flour and salt in a 2-quart mixing bowl, add eggs and whisk thoroughly. Add applesauce, lemon juice and grated rind and melted butter. Pour into pie shell and bake for about 1 hour or until lightly firm.

Note! *Pousse Café is a drink in which various liqueurs are poured carefully in order of their specific densities and the liquids remain in layers. By analogy I call this layered pie "Pousse Café".*

Pousse Café Tart

1 baked 9-inch pie shell, not deep dish
Lemon Curd, recipe follows
1/2 pint carton heavy whipping cream
Blueberry Sauce, recipe follows

In cooled pie shell make a layer of lemon curd no more than 1/2 inch deep, the curd is very rich. Whip the heavy cream. Carefully smooth the whipped cream over the curd layer to fill pie shell. Be careful not to mix the two! You want two distinct layers.

Place in refrigerator until served. When ready to serve, cut pie into 6 wedges and pour Blueberry Sauce over, don't overdo.

Lemon Curd

4 ounces butter, 1 stick
1 slightly heaping cup granulated sugar
3 large eggs
grated rind and juice of 2 lemons

Melt butter over very low heat and add sugar slowly and stir until well blended.

Beat eggs and add gradually to butter and sugar, stirring all the while. Do not allow to get very hot or butter will start to separate out and the mixture will look oily rather than creamy. Add lemon rind and juice, stirring in slowly. Continue to cook over low heat, stirring constantly, until the curd thickens and will coat the back of metal spoon. Test with instant-read thermometer to insure a temperature of 170°F. Cool and store in the refrigerator.

Blueberry Sauce

1/2 pint blueberries, fresh or frozen
sugar to taste about 1/2 cup
juice of 1/2 lemon

Heat berries until juices flow. Sweeten to taste and add lemon juice. Refrigerate. Can be used as dessert sauce or over waffles or pancakes.

Apple Puff

Serves 6 to 8

1 sheet frozen puff pastry dough, thawed
1 can (20 ounce) of unsweetened apples
1/2 cup light brown sugar, packed
1 teaspoon cinnamon
2 tablespoons butter
Preheat oven to 375°F

Melt butter in an 8-inch square pan and spread a layer of apples over the bottom. Sprinkle apples with sugar and cinnamon. Unfold pastry, gently, being careful not to stretch dough. Cut dough to fit as a lid and set it on top of apples. Bake on upper shelf of oven until dough is well browned and puffed, about 30 minutes. Serve warm with whipped cream or ice cream.

Lemon "Pseudo" Ice Box Pie

Serves 6 to 8

juice and zest of 2 large lemons—1/2 cup juice
9-inch, unbaked pie shell
1 can sweetened condensed milk
4 large eggs, separated
Preheat oven to 350°F

Beat egg whites until they are stiff but not dry. Set aside and in another bowl, combine condensed milk and egg yolks, mix them thoroughly. Gently stir in lemon juice and zest then fold in beaten whites. Put mixture in pie shell and bake for 50 minutes to 1 hour or until puffed and golden and internal temperature in center of pie is 170°F.

Chocolate Pie

Serves 6 to 8
4 large eggs
1 stick butter
1 1/3 cups sugar
3 ounces unsweetened chocolate, melted
1 teaspoon vanilla
1/2 cup walnuts or pecans
9-inch deep-dish pie shell, purchased frozen is fine
Preheat oven to 350°F

Cream butter and sugar as for a cake. Add eggs and beat then add melted chocolate and vanilla and stir in nuts. Pour into the unbaked pie shell and bake for about 50 minutes to 1 hour or until puffed and the internal temperature is 170°F.

Meringues

Serves 6
2 large eggs, separated
1/2 cup granulated sugar
1/2 teaspoon almond extract, optional
Preheat oven to 300°F

Be very certain that the metal bowl in which the whites will be beaten is absolutely free from even a trace of oil. Beat eggs at low speed until foamy. At a higher speed beat whites until stiff peaks are formed. Now, with the beater at the highest speed beat sugar and flavoring into the eggs adding the sugar a tablespoon at a time until all sugar is added and the mixture looks rather like marshmallow cream. Cover a cookie sheet with foil or wax paper and spray, very lightly, with pan spray then dust with cornstarch. Using heaping tablespoons of the mixture, doing one meringue at a time, put the mound on the prepared sheet and with the back of the spoon hollow out the centers and form a little rim all around the outside. Continue until all is used, make 6 shells. Do not allow them to touch. Place the sheet in the preheated oven and immediately lower the heat to 275°F. Bake for 30 minutes then turn oven off but allow the meringues to remain in the oven until it is cool or overnight. Serve filled with sweetened whipped cream and topped with berries or sliced peach or kiwi. Serve at once.

Strawberry Meringue

Serves 6
equivalent of 6 egg whites—use powdered, pasteurized egg white product
1 cup granulated sugar
Strawberry Filling
1 pint strawberries
1/2 pint heavy whipping cream
Preheat oven to 275°F

Reconstitute egg whites according to packet instructions. Gradually beat in 1 cup sugar until whites are a thick marshmallow cream-like mass. Using a 9-inch pie pan which can go to table. Heap the meringue into the pan and form into a rustic shell. Bake for about one hour until very lightly tan in color. Strawberry mix: Wash stem and slice berries thinly. Sweeten to taste. Whip cream stiffly, being careful not to over whip. Combine with strawberries, folding together gently. Allow shell to cool and heap strawberry mix into the shell immediately before serving.

Lemon Blueberry Pie

Serves 6 to 8

2/3 cup, fresh lemon juice (fresh juice is essential) this will be 4 to 6 lemons, depending on size

grated zest from 1 lemon (zest before cutting and squeezing, it's easier)

3 tablespoons of sour cream

5 large eggs

1 deep-dish 9-inch pie shell (purchased frozen will do nicely)

1 cup granulated sugar

1 cup fresh blueberries

Preheat oven to 350°F

Bake pie shell until lightly golden (about 10 minutes) and cool before adding remainder of ingredients. Rinse the blueberries and drain on paper towels then place in bottom of pie shell before adding lemon filling. In a large bowl whisk together the lemon juice, zest, sour cream and sugar until well blended and the sugar is dissolved. Beat in eggs, one at a time, beating thoroughly after each addition. Pour into pie shell that has been placed on a foil-lined baking pan, to prevent spills. Bake for about 30 minutes until lightly golden and firm. If in doubt about doneness, check temperature of pie with an "instant read" kitchen thermometer. The temperature in middle of filling in the center of the pie should be 170°F. At that temperature the eggs will be safe to eat. Cool before serving. A dollop of sour cream on each slice is a nice touch. This pie is very rich.

Note! This dessert is based on an English schoolboy dish named Eton Mess. It is very simple. The meringue, which is the rubble, can be made well in advance, and tightly wrapped. The remainder is simply whipped cream (which can be whipped several hours ahead and refrigerated) and strawberries. Toss all together at the last minute.

Rubble

Serves 6
1 pint heavy cream, whipped
1 pint strawberries, sliced, sugar them only if very tart
Meringue
4 egg whites
1 cup sugar
1 teaspoon vanilla
Preheat oven to 275°F

Beat egg whites until light and foamy, add vanilla and gradually beat in sugar until the whites are thick and shiny and stand in peaks when beater is lifted. Line a baking sheet with waxed paper, spray with pan spray and dust with cornstarch. Drop mounds of meringue and flatten slightly. Bake for about 1 hour. Can be baked ahead and kept sealed in plastic bag.

A few minutes before serving, crumble meringues into whipped cream and fold in berries. This is very rich so give small servings.

Gourmet Alert! *This is the best pecan pie I have ever eaten. My mother gave me the recipe. Unlike most pecan pies, this one is not overly sweet and it has lots of nuts. Try this with a cup of strong coffee.*

Pecan Pie

Serves 6 to 8
1 cup white corn syrup
1/2 cup light brown sugar, packed
1/4 teaspoon salt
1 teaspoon vanilla
2 teaspoons fresh lemon juice
3 large eggs
1 1/2 cups pecan halves or pieces
1 purchased 9-inch deep-dish pie shell or homemade 9-inch
Preheat oven to 400°F

Break eggs into mixing bowl and beat lightly. Add next five ingredients and combine thoroughly. Add pecans and stir. Pour into piecrust and place in oven. Bake 10 minutes and then reduce heat to 325°F and bake 30 to 35 minutes or until crust is golden and filling set. Allow to cool thoroughly before serving.

Note! *I usually recommend frozen pie dough, because it's good and saves time. But if you are going to bake pecan pie by the recipe above, you might as well bake it in this great piecrust below.*

Pie Crust

Serves 6 to 8

2 cups all-purpose flour, sifted before measuring
1 stick butter (4 ounce), very cold or frozen and cut into bits
1/2 teaspoon salt about 3 ounces cold water
Preheat oven to 375°F

In a food processor pulse the flour, butter and salt until it resembles corn meal. Add water gradually until the dough forms a ball. Don't get it too wet. This is enough for a double crust 9-inch pie or 3 (9-inch) flan shells. Roll on well-floured wax paper or parchment until of appropriate size. Turn the dough often so it doesn't stretch. Fold the dough in half, place in piepan, and unfold. Pat carefully into place. Trim or crimp edges around rim. Refrigerate unused dough.

Walnut Tart (Flan)

Serves 6 to 8

2 large eggs
2 cups walnuts
3/4 cup white white corn syrup
1/2 cup sugar
3 tablespoon butter, melted
1 tablespoon orange juice
zest of 1/2 orange
9-inch flan shell, directions below

In a large mixing bowl whisk the eggs and sugar together and then stir in remainder of ingredients. Bake in 9-inch flan shell. See below. When shell is ready, fill with the walnut mixture and bake at 330°F for about 40 minutes or until golden and center is slightly puffed.

Flan Shell (9-inch)

Heat oven to 375°F. Use a flan pan with loose bottom. Roll pastry (Pie Crust recipe above) on well-floured wax paper or parchment until of appropriate size. Turn the dough often so it doesn't stretch. Fit the dough carefully into the pan, without tearing it. If you do tear it, mend with dough moistened with water. Fit a foil sheet over dough and put in a thin layer of rice. Bake for about 10 minutes. Remove from oven, remove foil and allow shell to cool.

Pear and Mincemeat Flan

Blond Mincemeat, recipe this Chapter
1/3 cup walnuts
1 large ripe but firm Bosc pear
1 (9-inch) flan shell, see previous recipe
Preheat oven to 330°F

Use a flan pan with loose bottom. Roll Pie Crust (recipe this Chapter) dough on well-floured wax paper or parchment until of appropriate size. Turn the dough often so it doesn't stretch. Fit the dough carefully into the pan, without tearing it. If you do tear it, mend with dough moistened with water. Trim dough around top of sides, so there is no overhang. Spread a thin layer of mincemeat over bottom of shell, being careful not to damage the pastry. Peel and core pear and cut it into thin, lengthwise slices. Arrange the slices, large side toward center in a fan on the mincemeat. Place a few walnuts between each pear slice. Cover pear and walnuts with a layer of mincemeat that fills the pan to the top. Bake for about 40 minutes. The fruit will be lightly caramelized. Don't let it get past golden or it will taste bitter. If necessary, cover top with foil to finish baking.

Pineapple Tarts

Serves 6

6 uncooked, purchased puff pastry patty shells, thawed
6 drained canned pineapple slices
light brown sugar to sprinkle
1 cup light brown sugar, packed
1/3 cup heavy cream
Preheat oven to 400°F

Using the pineapple slices as a guide, flatten the patty shells with your fingers, so there is a border of dough about 1/8 inch around each slice of pineapple. Lightly sprinkle each dough circle with sugar and lay pineapple over. On a foil-lined baking sheet just large enough to accommodate the rounds when lightly touching, bake for about 15 minutes until rounds are puffed and golden.

In a small pan, combine the cream and 1 cup sugar and stir while heating until sugar is dissolved. Bring to a light boil and remove from heat immediately. This makes a nice sauce for the pastries.

Cheesecake Strawberry Pie

Serves 6 to 8
1 purchased pie shell (9-inch)
1 package (8 ounce) cream cheese
1/3 cup heavy cream
1/3 cup granulated sugar
1 teaspoon vanilla
1 pint fresh strawberries
1 cup currant or strawberry jelly

Bake the pie shell according to package directions and cool. In a metal bowl, beat the cream cheese, cream, sugar and vanilla until well mixed and smooth. Gently smooth the cheese mixture into the pie shell. Wash the strawberries, remove caps and pat the berries dry. Arrange the berries, points up, on the cheese mixture. In a small saucepan, melt the jelly over very low heat until just melted. Allow the jelly to cool slightly and then spoon it evenly over the berries and cheese. Refrigerate until serving time.

Pineapple Puff

Serves 6
1 medium pineapple
1/2 cup light brown sugar, packed
1/2 teaspoon cinnamon
1 sheet purchased puff pastry dough, thawed
Preheat oven to 375°F

Peel and core pineapple and cut into dice. Put pineapple into baking dish (a 9-inch pie plate works well). Sprinkle fruit with the sugar and cinnamon. Before filling baking dish, invert it on the pastry and use it as a template for measuring the top. Check dough size to insure that it covers baking dish, gently rolling it to enlarge it if necessary. Cover the dish with the pastry, tucking the edges into the dish down along the sides. Bake at for about 35 to 40 minutes or until top is well browned.

<u>Gourmet Alert!</u> *This is a beautiful as well as delicious tart. It's great for special occasions.*

Apricot Tart

Serves 6 to 8
1 purchased pie shell (9-inch) not deep dish
1 pound fresh apricots
1 package (8 ounce) cream cheese
1/4 cup heavy cream or sour cream
1/4 cup granulated sugar
1 large egg
1/2 teaspoon pure vanilla
3/4 cup apricot jam
1/4 cup sliced almonds
Preheat oven to 350°F

Bake pie shell for 5 minutes. Place pie shell on a foil lined baking pan. In a bowl beat together thoroughly the cream cheese, cream (if using sour cream increase sugar by 1 tablespoon), sugar, egg and vanilla. Spread this mixture in the bottom of the pie shell. Rinse and drain the apricots and split and remove pits. Place the apricot halves on the cheese mixture, cut side up. Don't crowd the halves, they shouldn't touch. Melt the apricot jam and spoon over and around the fruit. Sprinkle the almonds over. Bake for 15 minutes then reduce the heat to 325°F and bake for 45 minutes longer. Allow to cool so the cheese mixture can solidify before serving. The pie is very rich. Serve in small pieces.

<u>Note</u>! Here is a dessert ingredient you may not have heard of. dulce de leche means, roughly, sweet milk. It is a semi-soft caramel and is very rich. The best dulce de leche is made in Argentina and can be bought in many Latin markets.

Dulce de Leche Tart

Serves 6 to 8
2/3 cup purchased dulce de leche (a caramel confection sold in jars at many Latin markets)
1/3 cup heavy cream
2 large eggs
1/4 cup light brown sugar, packed
1 teaspoon vanilla
1/4 teaspoon ground cinnamon
1 cup nuts, pecans or lightly toasted sliced almonds
1 purchased 9-inch pie shell
Preheat oven to 350°F

Bake pie shell for 5 minutes. Remove from oven. In separate bowl, combine first six ingredients and mix thoroughly. Stir in nuts and pour mixture into pie shell. Place pie shell onto foil-lined baking pan. Bake for about 30 minutes or until the pie is puffed and golden. Cool to room temperature before serving in small slices.

Banana Cheesecake Tart

Serves 6 to 8
1 purchased pie shell, (9-inch), not deep dish
1 package (8 ounce) cream cheese
1/4 cup heavy cream or sour cream
1/4 cup granulated sugar
1 large egg
1/2 teaspoon pure vanilla
3/4 cup dulce de leche (a caramel confection sold in jars at many Latin markets)*
2 large bananas, yellow but not showing brown spots
Preheat oven to 350°F

Bake pie shell for 5 minutes. Place pie shell on a foil lined baking pan. Beat together well, the cream cheese, cream (if using sour cream increase sugar by 1 tablespoon), sugar, egg and vanilla. Bake for 15 minutes then reduce the heat to 325°F and bake for 45 minutes longer. Allow to cool. Then peel and slice bananas and place slices neatly over pie. Heat the dulce de leche until it flows easily then spread over and between banana slices. Chill so the topping can solidify before serving. The pie is very rich. Serve in small pieces. Refrigerate any leftovers.

*Dulce Substitute—Melt 30 Hershey's Caramels with 1/3 cup heavy cream.

Upside Down Pudding

Serves 4 to 6

Fruit Layer

1/2 cup light brown sugar, packed

3/4 stick butter, softened

2 cups fruits and nuts (see note below)*

Cake Layer

3/4 stick butter

1/2 cup granulated sugar

2 large eggs

1 teaspoon vanilla

1/4 cup milk

1 1/2 cups self-rising flour

Preheat oven to 350°F

To make fruit layer, oil, or spray with pan spray, bottom and sides of 8-inch diameter, round or square baking pan. Cream sugar and butter and spread in bottom of pan. Arrange fruits/nuts over sugar layer in neat pattern.

To make cake, cream butter, sugar and vanilla together. Add eggs and milk and beat well. Fold in flour and spread carefully over fruit. Bake for 30 to 35 minutes or until done. Allow pan to rest for about 10 minutes then place a plate over the pan and carefully invert. Remove pan and scrape out any remaining fruit bits and sugar and carefully replace on cake. Serve warm with cream or ice cream.

***Fruits and Nuts**: Use as desired to make 2 cups, your choice, but use some nuts such as walnuts or pecans, dried apricots, plums or prunes lightly soaked as needed to soften.

Lemon Curd

1 stick butter
1 heaping cup granulated sugar
3 large eggs
grated rind and juice of 2 lemons

Melt butter over very low heat and add sugar slowly and stir until well blended.

In separate bowl, beat eggs and add gradually to butter and sugar, stirring all the while. Do not allow to get very hot or butter will start to separate out and the mixture will look oily rather than creamy. Add lemon rind and juice, stirring in slowly. Continue to cook over low heat, stirring constantly, until the curd thickens and will coat the back of metal spoon. Test with instant-read thermometer to insure a temperature of 170°F. Cool and store in the refrigerator.

Blueberry Sauce

1/2 pint blueberries, fresh or frozen
sugar to taste about 1/2 cup
juice of 1/2 lemon

Heat berries until juices flow. Sweeten to taste and add lemon juice. Refrigerate. Can be used as dessert sauce or over waffles or pancakes.

Baked Chocolate Filled Pears with Custard

Serves 4
4 fresh, ripe pears
4 tablespoons (approximately) tiny semi-sweet chocolate morsels
2 teaspoons whipping cream or half & half
4 heaping teaspoons granulated sugar
1 packet of custard mix (Prepared according to packet instructions, Bird's for preference)
Preheat oven to 350°F

Peel and core pears and place in shallow baking dish. Fill the cored centers with the chocolate bits and add about 2 teaspoon of cream or half & half, sprinkle each pear with a heaping teaspoon of granulated sugar. Cover the baking dish tightly with aluminum foil and bake for about 20 minutes or until the pears pierce easily with a knife. Serve with warm custard poured over.

Lemon Custard Pudding

Serves 6
zest and juice of 4 lemons
1 stick softened butter
1 1/2 cups granulated sugar
4 large eggs, separated
1/4 cup all-purpose flour
1/2 cup milk
Preheat oven to 350°F

Butter an 8-inch soufflé dish or gratin. Beat the egg whites until they are firm and stand in peaks. Set aside and in another bowl cream the butter and sugar until well blended and add the lemon zest and juice. The mixture will probably separate at this juncture but not to worry. Beat in the egg yolks thoroughly and then beat in flour and milk, starting and ending with flour. Fold in the egg whites, gently but thoroughly. Pour into buttered baking dish and place dish in baking pan and pour water into the pan so the baking dish will be sitting in water half way up the sides. Bake for about 1 hour or until the top is golden and the temperature in the center is 170°F. Serve warm or at room temperature.

Zippy Peach Pudding

Serves 6 to 8

1 package (12 ounce) frozen peach slices or 4 cups peeled, sliced fresh peaches

1/2 cup granulated sugar

1 teaspoon cinnamon

1 pinch cayenne pepper

Cake Topping:

1 stick butter

1 1/3 cups granulated sugar

3 large eggs

1/2 cup milk

2 cups sifted self-rising flour

2 teaspoons vanilla

Preheat oven to 350°F

In a small saucepan, heat the peaches only until juice begins to run, then stir in 1/2 cup sugar, cinnamon and cayenne. Set aside. Cream the butter and sugar (if the butter isn't at room temperature, microwave it for about 15 seconds). Add the eggs and vanilla and beat thoroughly. Beat in flour and milk, alternately starting and ending with flour. Butter or spray with pan spray a roughly 10 inch x 10 inch or 8 inch x 12 inch pan. Pour the peaches into the bottom of the pan and pour the cake batter over, smoothing top. Bake for about 50 minutes or until the top is golden and a pick inserted into the cake comes out clean. Serve warm or at room temperature.

Mama's Bread Pudding

Serves 6 to 8
12 slices cinnamon raisin bread, toasted and buttered
1/2 cup granulated sugar
3 tablespoons granulated sugar
3 large eggs, beaten
3 cups milk, heated
1 teaspoon vanilla
Preheat oven to 350°F

Butter or spray with pan spray a baking dish roughly 8 x 10 x 2 or a 9-inch round about 2 inches deep. Cut the buttered raisin toasts to form two layers in the pan. Beat the eggs with the 1/2 cup sugar and vanilla and add the hot milk, whisking gently all the while. Pour the mixture over the toasts and push down the bread so that all has been covered with the milk mix. When most of the milk has been absorbed, about 10 minutes, sprinkle the pudding with the remaining 2 tablespoons sugar and place the baking dish in the oven. Bake for about 30 minutes or until well-puffed and golden brown. Good hot, warm, or cold. Great with ice cream or warm custard.

<u>Note</u>*! The next recipe is a very popular southern dessert. It is properly pronounced "Banana Puddin'".*

Banana Pudding

4 to 5 ripe, medium bananas
2 packets Bird's custard powder, or other available brand
4 cups whole milk
25 to 30 vanilla wafers (use ones made with real vanilla)

Make pudding according to packet directions cover and refrigerate until cool. Using an attractive five-pint glass dish, make a layer of wafers then pudding and then layer sliced bananas. Keep making layers to use up ingredients, finishing with a pudding layer on top.

Blueberry Crumble Pudding

Serves 6 to 8
2 pints fresh blueberries
1/2 cup brown sugar, packed
1/2 cup granulated sugar
1 teaspoon cinnamon
1 1/2 cups all-purpose flour
1 stick butter
juice of 1 lemon
Preheat oven to 375°F

Combine granulated sugar, cinnamon, lemon juice and 3 tablespoon of the flour and mix with the blueberries. Pour into a buttered or oiled 10 x 6 x 2 inch or equivalent size baking dish. Combine brown sugar, flour and butter and work together until nicely blended into crumbs. Sprinkle over berry mixture evenly. Bake about 1 hour or until bubbling and golden brown.

Caramelized Pineapple with Coconut Custard

Serves 6
first make Coconut Custard and refrigerate
1 medium pineapple
1 cup light brown sugar, packed
1 1/2 tablespoons butter

Peel and core the pineapple and cut it into bite-size wedges. In a heavy, non-reactive medium size skillet, melt the butter and add the pineapple and sugar. Cook and occasionally stir over medium heat for about 15 minutes or until the pineapple has quit giving off juice and the sauce has thickened. Serve with custard poured over.

Coconut Custard

1 packet Bird's or other brand custard powder
1 can (13.5 ounce) unsweetened coconut milk
1/4 cup milk (or a total of 2 cups of coconut and regular milk)
1 teaspoon vanilla
1/4 cup granulated sugar.

Follow packet directions for preparation, but use ingredients above. If you use a can of coconut milk larger than 13.5 ounces, use only enough regular milk to bring total liquid to 2 cups (16 ounces).

<u>Note</u>! *I developed this next recipe to be a cross between a strawberry short cake and a mousse, whence the name.*

Strawberry Short Mousse

Serves 6

chocolate cake (see recipe this chapter)
1 pint heavy whipping cream
1/4 cup granulated sugar
1 teaspoon vanilla
1/2 pint of strawberries, sliced, reserving one berry

Bake cake and allow to cool thoroughly before proceeding. The cake may be baked a day or two before using and sealed tightly in a plastic bag. To assemble: Place cake on serving platter and carefully remove the center portion of the cake preserving the bottom and a rim about 1/2 inch deep around sides. Whip the cream until stiff and add sugar and vanilla then beat until very stiff, being careful not to over beat because the cream will turn into butter. Set aside about 1/4 cup of the whipped cream. Crumble enough cake to make about 1 cup crumbs and fold crumbs into the larger portion of whipped cream. Fold in the strawberries and pile into the cake case. Top with the reserved cream and strawberry.

Cheesecake New York Style

Serves 12

2 pounds cream cheese (not low fat)
1 cup granulated sugar
3 large eggs
1 teaspoon pure vanilla extract
2 tablespoons all-purpose flour
1 cup sour cream
zest and juice of 1 lemon or lime
(2 may be used for more intense flavor)
pan spray
1/2 cup vanilla cookie crumbs
1 spring form pan, 9-inch
Topping below
Preheat oven to 350°F

In a large metal bowl beat cream cheese and sugar until blended. Beat in the eggs, one at a time, then add vanilla, citrus zest and juice and flour until thoroughly mixed. Beat in sour cream until thoroughly blended. During the beating process scrape down sides of bowl. Spray bottom and sides of pan thoroughly and add crumbs. Shake and rotate pan until bottom and sides are lightly coated. Remaining crumbs will settle to bottom of pan. Fill pan with cheese mixture. Set pan on cookie sheet.

Bake for 20 minutes. Reduce heat to 300° F and bake for 1 1/2 hours or until lightly golden around sides and center is no longer liquid. It is wise to test with an instant read thermometer to insure that temperature has reached 170° F, at which time the eggs will be thoroughly cooked. Turn off the heat. Allow the cake to cool in the oven with the door propped open for 1 to 2 hours. Refrigerate for at least 3 hours before serving. Just before serving, remove sides from pan, and spread topping.

Topping for Cheese Cake

approximately 1 cup each of sour cream and apricot jam

Before serving, make border of jam about 1 inch wide around the outside of the top of the cake, and cover the remainder of the top with sour cream.

Upside Down Ginger Pear Cake

Ginger Cake

Serves 6 to 8
1 1/4 cups all-purpose flour
1/2 teaspoon, bicarbonate of soda (baking soda)
2 teaspoons cinnamon
2 teaspoons ground dried ginger
1/2 stick butter
1 large egg
1/2 cup light brown sugar, packed
1/2 cup mild molasses
1/2 cup milk
Preheat oven to 350°F

Mix dry ingredients. In separate bowl, melt butter and add to sugar, molasses, milk and egg. Stir liquids into dry ingredients and mix well.

Make Topping for Ginger Cake (recipe below). Gently pour cake batter over topping (which is, of course, the bottom while baking). Bake for 45 to 50 minutes or until done. After removing from oven, allow to sit for about 10 minutes then cover with plate and carefully turn over and remove pan. If any pears or sugar remain in pan, remove carefully and put on cake.

Topping for Ginger Cake

1/2 stick butter
1/2 cup light brown sugar, packed
1 can (15 ounce) pears in fruit juice or water, drained
1/2 cup walnuts or pecans

Melt butter and combine with brown sugar. Pour into 8-in round or square pan and sprinkle with nuts and drained pears, each half divided into half lengthwise. Put pears with rounded side toward bottom of pan and small end (stem end) toward center of pan.

Coconut Macaroons

Makes about 20 Macaroons
2 egg whites, from large eggs
1/4 cup granulated sugar
1/2 teaspoon vanilla
1 to 1 1/2 cups sweetened coconut
Preheat oven to 300°F

Be very certain that the metal bowl in which the whites will be beaten is absolutely free from even a trace of oil. Beat eggs at low speed until foamy. At a higher speed beat whites until stiff peaks are formed. Now, with the beater at the highest speed beat sugar and flavoring into the eggs adding the sugar a tablespoon at a time until all sugar is added and the mixture looks rather like marshmallow cream. Fold in coconut. Cover a cookie sheet with foil or wax paper and spray, very lightly, with pan spray then dust with cornstarch. Spoon tablespoons of meringue into mounds on the cookiesheet. Bake until golden, about 30 minutes.

Chocolate Walnut Cake

Serves 6 to 8
1 stick plus 2 tablespoons (5 ounces) butter
1/2 cup light brown sugar, packed and slightly heaped
2 large eggs
1 cup self-rising flour
1/2 cup semi-sweet chocolate bits
1/2 cup walnut or pecan pieces
1 tablespoon strong coffee
Preheat oven to 350°F

In a metal or plastic bowl, cream butter and sugar. Beat in eggs then stir in flour and coffee. Stir in chocolate and nuts. Oil and line with greased waxed paper, an 8-inch diameter baking pan. Pour in batter and bake for about 25 minutes or until a knife inserted in center comes out clean. Rest in pan for about 10 minutes then invert on plate. Good warm or cold.

Mango Meringue Cake

Serves 6 to 8
equivalent of 6 egg whites—use powdered, pasteurized egg white product
1 cup granulated sugar
Mango Filling
2 mangoes, peeled and sliced, reserve 1 slice
1 cup heavy cream, whipped
Preheat oven to 275°F

Reconstitute egg whites according to packet instructions. Gradually beat in 1 cup sugar, until whites are a thick marshmallow cream-like mass. Using a 9-inch plate draw two circles on waxed paper. Place the wax paper on a cookie sheet. Spray lightly with pan spray. Spread 1/2 of meringue on each circle. Bake for about one hour until very lightly tan in color. While the meringue is still somewhat pliable, remove carefully from paper by sticking a spatula under to loosen. Put one circle on serving dish and spread 2/3 of the whipped cream over then the mango. Top with the other meringue and heap the reserved cream in the center. Garnish with a mango slice.

Mango Upside-Down Cake

Serves 6 to 8
2 mangoes, peeled and sliced
1/3 cup butter, (5 1/3 tablespoons)
1/2 cup granulated sugar
Cake
1 cup self-rising flour
pinch of cinnamon
2 large eggs
2/3 cup sugar
1/4 cup milk
1 teaspoon vanilla
Preheat oven to 350°F

In a heavy 9-in or 10-in round pan melt butter and 1/2 cup sugar. Sprinkle with cinnamon and mix and smooth in bottom of pan. Make a layer of mango over the sugar, butter mix. In separate bowl, whisk eggs and sugar and add vanilla. Add half of flour and whisk inch Add milk then whisk in remaining flour. Pour over fruit. Bake for about 20 minutes or until a toothpick inserted in center comes out clean, Allow the cake to rest for about 10 minutes then CAREFULLY place over top and invert. Remove pan. If any of the topping sticks to the pan, then scoop it out and spread where it is needed.

Banana Shortcake

Cake

Serves 6 to 8

1 stick (4 ounce) butter
1 1/3 cups light brown sugar, packed
3 large eggs
1/2 cup milk
2 cups sifted self-rising flour
2 teaspoons vanilla
Preheat oven to 350°F

Cream the butter and sugar (if the butter isn't at room temperature, microwave it for about 15 seconds). Add the eggs and vanilla and beat thoroughly. Beat in flour and milk, alternately in parts, starting and ending with flour. Spray with pan spray an 8-inch x 12-inch pan. Bake for about 50 minutes or until the top is golden and a pick inserted into the cake comes out clean.

Topping

3 large ripe bananas
1 pint heavy cream
1/2 cup granulated sugar
1 teaspoon vanilla

Shortly before serving, whip cream with sugar and vanilla until very stiff, be careful not to over beat. Slice cooled cake in half horizontally through middle to form two thin layers. Spread cut side with cream and sliced banana, place second layer over and spread cream and banana on top. Refrigerate uneaten portion.

Blueberry Cheesecake

Serves 8 to 10

3 packages (8 ounce each) of cream cheese (not low fat)
1 cup vanilla wafer crumbs
3/4 cup granulated sugar
2 tablespoons flour
4 large eggs
2/3 cup sour cream (not low fat), plus additional for frosting
1 teaspoon vanilla extract
1/2 teaspoon cinnamon
1 lemon, zest and juice
1 cup blueberries, reserve 3 or 4
Preheat oven to 350°F

Oil a 9-inch springform pan and spread a layer of vanilla wafer crumbs evenly over the bottom. Wrap foil around the bottom and sides of pan and set it on a cookie sheet. Combine cream cheese, sugar and flour in a large bowl, metal or plastic, and beat until smooth with an electric mixer. Add eggs and beat well. Stir in sour cream, vanilla and lemon. Fold in blueberries and pour over crumbs in pan. Bake for 15 minutes. Reduce temperature to 225° and bake for about 1 hour or until the center no longer looks liquid and soft. The temperature in the center should be 170°. Run a knife around the side of the pan to free the cake from the side. Chill in the refrigerator for several hours or overnight.

Remove sides of pan. If the top has cracked, don't worry, Spread sour cream over as "frosting" and garnish with blueberries. Refrigerate uneaten portion.

Snow White and Rose Red

Serves 8
1 pint heavy whipping cream
1/3 cup granulated sugar
1 teaspoon vanilla
2/3 of a small purchased angel food cake, torn into pieces
1 pint strawberries, sliced, reserve 1 or 2 for garnish

Whip cream with sugar and vanilla until stiff. Refrigerate. Immediately before serving, mix all ingredients together in an attractive glass bowl and garnish with reserved berries. Serve in small amounts since this is very rich. Refrigerate uneaten portion.

Quick Cheese Cakes

Serves 6
6 Pepperidge Farm puff patty shells
1 package (8 ounce) cream cheese
1 egg
1/2 teaspoon vanilla
1/3 cup granulated sugar
Preheat oven to 300°F

Bake patty shells according to package directions. When done, remove lids. The directions tell how to do this. Beat cheese, egg, vanilla and sugar together until smooth. Fill each pastry about 1/2 full and bake on foil-lined baking sheet for about 30 minutes. Serve with whipped cream and fresh fruit.

Chocolate Cake

Serves 8 to 10
5 large eggs
1 cup plus 2 tablespoons granulated sugar
4 ounces plus 1 tablespoon salted butter,
4 1/2 ounces unsweetened chocolate
1 teaspoon vanilla
1 cup sifted all-purpose flour
Preheat oven to 350° F

Melt the chocolate and butter together either in the microwave or in a small bowl over simmering water, don't let the water touch the bowl. Set aside. Separate eggs and beat whites until they are stiff but not dry. Set aside. Beat the egg yolks and sugar until thick and lemon colored, beat in vanilla. Beat in the melted chocolate and butter. Beat in the flour a bit at a time. Carefully fold in the egg whites. Line an 8-inch baking pan with foil, smoothing the folds and spray with pan spray. Pour in cake batter and bake for about 30 minutes or until a toothpick inserted in the center comes out clean. Cool cake and remove from pan and remove foil.

Very Chocolate Cake

Serves 8 to 10
9 ounces (1 1/2 cups) semi-sweet chocolate bits
6 ounces butter
1 tablespoon Bourbon whiskey
4 large eggs
2/3 cup granulated sugar
1 cup plus 2 tablespoons self-rising flour
3 ounces almonds, ground, a well-rounded 1/2 cup
Preheat the oven to 350°F

Melt the chocolate and butter together in the microwave or in a bowl set over a pan of gently boiling water, making sure the water doesn't touch the bowl. When melted, remove the bowl from the heat source and stir in the Bourbon then allow the mixture to cool for about 5 minutes. Combine the eggs and sugar in a mixing bowl and beat with a mixer or whisk until thick and lemon colored. Add the chocolate mixture to the eggs and sugar and mix well. Finally fold in the flour and almonds gently but thoroughly. Pour into oiled and floured 9 inch round baking pan. Bake for 45 minutes or until a toothpick inserted into the center of the cake comes out clean. Cool for about 15 minutes then run a knife or spatula around the side of the tin to release cake and turn out on a plate. Allow to cool thoroughly before frosting with chocolate ganache frosting below. Slice cake to make two layers before filling and frosting.

Chocolate Ganache Frosting

9 ounces (1 1/2 cups) semi-sweet chocolate bits
1 cup heavy cream
1 teaspoon vanilla

Bring the cream to a simmer then turn the chocolate into the cream and stir until the chocolate is melted. Beat until the mixture begins to thicken and then allow to cool completely at which time the mixture will be quite thick. This is enough to fill and frost the "Very Chocolate Cake."

Tropical Ice Cream

Serves 16
1 half gallon good quality vanilla ice cream
1 or 2 mangoes (depending on size and how fond you are of mangoes)
2 medium bananas
1 cup sweetened shredded coconut

Remove ice cream from carton and place into a large bowl. Allow to soften but not get mushy. Wash mangoes then peel and chop, combine with coconut and fold into ice cream. Turn into a freezer container and refreeze before serving.

Chocolate Pie Ice Cream

Serves 16 to 20
1/4 chocolate pie (recipe this chapter)
1/2 gallon vanilla ice cream

Crumble pie and combine with ice cream. Store in freezer.

Mango, Strawberry Sundae

Serves 8

1 pint strawberries, save 4 for garnish, purée remainder
2 mangoes, peeled and sliced
sugar
1 quart vanilla ice cream

Purée strawberries and sweeten to taste. For each sundae, put a spoonful or two of the strawberry purée in the bottom of a dish add 2 scoops of vanilla ice cream then add mango slices and remainder of purée. Garnish with saved berries.

Glossary

Amandine — A method of food preparation which involves sautéing the food in butter and sprinkling with almonds which have also been sautéed in butter.

Arrabbiata — A spicy Italian tomato sauce. Try the recipe in the Dressings and Sauces Chapter.

Balsamic Vinegar — An aged grape vinegar which is dark and somewhat sweet.

Béchamel — A classic French white sauce. Try the recipe in the Dressings and Sauces Chapter.

Blanch — Literally, this means to remove the color, or whiten. In cooking it means to place food (usually vegetables) in boiling water for a very short time (1 or 2 minutes). This just barely sets the color of the vegetables, without softening them. They should still be crisp. Refresh them in cold or ice water.

Bruschetta — An classic Italian dish made with a slice of bread, spread with olive oil and garlic. It can be plain or have toppings. Now it is even applied to desserts using a slice of sweet bread as the base.

Buerre Manie	This is a mixture of equal parts of butter and flour. It must be thoroughly mixed and creamed. It is used to add to sauces to further thicken them when other thickening agents were insufficient. Buerre manie can be kept for extended periods in the refrigerator, handy for use when needed.
Buttermilk	Originally, buttermilk was the milk left over after making butter. Now it is low fat milk to which a harmless culture has been added to sour it.
Cacciatora	It means "hunter style": meat, chicken or fish cooked in a rich sauce which, among other things, includes tomatoes, peppers and mushrooms.
Chicken Tenders	Strips of breast of chicken, just a good size for frying quickly.
Chop	A small portion of meat cut from the rib, for sautéing or broiling.
Cobbler	A type of preparation which has cobbles in it. Cobbles are small bits shaped like the stones with which streets were paved in the days of sailing ships because they were ballast and therefore readily available. In food preparation, cobbles are small clumps of dough cooked on the dish as a topping.
Cobbles	The small biscuits shaped like paving stones topping cobblers.
Cordon Bleu	A name for a type of food preparation which involves a main ingredient, such as veal or chicken, enhanced with ham and cheese. See one of the Cordon Bleu recipes in this book.
Cottage Pie	A meat pie (usually not lamb) which is topped

	with potatoes, rather than crust. See also "Shepherd's Pie".
Cream	As a verb the word means to thoroughly mix together ingredients into a "cream-like" consistency
Cream	As a noun the word refers to the fatty portion of milk, that rises to the top of milk that is not homogenized. Cream is sold in all supermarkets in several levels of butterfat content, or richness. The least butterfat is in half & half and in ascending order of butterfat there is table cream, whipping cream, and heavy whipping cream. In the recipes in this book you will not find table cream. I do specify which type of cream is needed in the recipes, and it is important to use the right cream. For thickening sauces, I will generally specify half & half or cream, by which I mean whipping cream. That is because half & half is rich enough that it will not curdle in the acid of a sauce, whereas, milk would. For whipping I specify heavy whipping cream because it will actually whip successfully, whereas whipping cream may or may not.

Type of product	% of Butterfat
whole milk	4
half & half	>10.5
light cream	18-30
whipping cream	30-36
heavy whipping cream	36-40

See also Evaporated Milk, Buttermilk and Sour cream

Crustades	Toasted crusts of bread, Small ones are called croutons.
Cutlet	A small portion of meat cut from the leg or rib for broiling or sautéing. It is also called a chop if cut from the rib. See "chop"

Deglaze   Deglazing is done by adding liquid to a pan which has been used for sautéing, in order to soften the juices and crispy bits clinging to the pan, thus making the foundation for a sauce.

Dice   Chop into cubes

Dulche de Leche   A sweet thick syrup made from milk and sugar. It is caramel-like. It is grand in some pies. Try one of the Dulce de Leche recipes in this book.

Dressing   Usually means a liquid collection of ingredients to be poured over a salad. Can also mean a stuffing for poultry or meat, except that I recommend that you not put the dressing in the turkey (don't "stuff" it) but cook the dressing (stuffing) on the side. It cooks better and does not absorb more of the fat than you put in it. It is also safer because it is easier to cook to a high enough temperature, without overcooking the bird.

Dumpling   A small mass of dough cooked by boiling in a soup, gravy or syrup. There are also baked, usually fruit, dumplings made with a covering of pastry. Try one of the recipes in this book. See also "Spaetzele".

Evaporated Milk   Evaporated milk is milk which has had it's water content reduced by half, in a vacuum, not by boiling. It is then sterilized. Sweetened condensed milk is evaporated, sterilized milk which is sweetened so that its composition is 1/5 sugar.

Flour   All purpose flour is a blend of hard and soft wheats ground into a fine powder. Self-rising flour is all purpose flour to which salt and double acting baking powder has been added. Double acting means activated by moisture and by heat. In self-rising flour the ingredients are more thoroughly mixed then can be done by sifting, and therefore gives a better result. Also the proportions are exact in self-rising flour, and therefore the results are the same every time. It's use simplifies the preparation of biscuits, and other types of non-yeast doughs.

If you cannot easily get self-rising flour, you can make an approximation to it by adding 1 tablespoon of baking powder and 1 teaspoon of salt for 2 cups of all-purpose flour.

Fool — A dessert of fruit and whipped cream. See many recipes in this book.

Fry — This literally means to immerse completely in very hot fat to cook. That is, of course, what has come to be called deep-fat frying. The man (or woman) on the street understands frying to mean putting food in a layer of fat in a skillet, turning as necessary, and cooking. That really is sautéing. No need to be a stickler, but we do need to communicate! See "sauté".

Garlic — This is a member of the onion, allium, family. It is a bulb which is a collection of segments, called cloves. If you purchase it fresh, look for plump, heavy bulbs with no browning or mold. It's shelf life is relatively short because it tends to dry up. It is also available as a purée or chopped in jars, which need to be refrigerated after they are opened. Dry ground garlic (granulated) in coarse and fine (garlic powder) grinds are also available. The coarse (or granulated) is easier to use as it does not scatter as easily as the powdered form.

Goujonettes — Little bits about the size and shape as the European fish, goujon. In reference to chicken, these are like chicken tenders, namely, strips of chicken breast.

Gratin	A type of pan in which a casserole is made. It is usually oblong or round. The word also refires to the type of food product made in the pan, namely, a casserole.
Gravy	The thickened juices of some food. See "sauce".
Ham Glaze	A topping for a piece of ham. Also as a verb, to put the topping on the ham.
Hot Sauce	Hot sauces are made from ground hot peppers (capsicum), mixed with vinegar and salt. They have many uses. Crystal tends to be relatively mild, and is more tolerant toward experimenting in cooking, whereas, Tabasco is quite hot and may be your choice when a little is being added at the table, where quantities can be carefully controlled individually.
Kedgeree	A preparation of fish using curry and many other ingredients. Kedgerees vary greatly as to seasonings and ingredients. This dish was popularized in Great Britan through its long association with India. It is a marriage of cultures.
Marchand de Vin	A classic French sauce (it means wine merchant's sauce). As used in this book, it is very much a New Orleans version of the French sauce. See the recipe in the Dressings and Sauces Chapter.
Marinate	To let rest in a seasoning liquid, generally one which will tenderize the food. The word appears to have come from letting the food lie in brine, as from the sea.
Mirleton	mirleton is a type of squash about the size of a

	large avocado. It is soft green in color, much like the color of Iceberg lettuce, and very wrinkled.
Mistral	A way of preparing food which is very strongly garlic seasoned. How it comes by the name is a mystery to me. The word literally means a violent, cold, and dry, northerly wind in the Mediterranean provinces of France. Go figure.
Mustard	Mustard is a member of the same family, brasseia, as cabbage and broccoli. The seeds of the mustard plant are ground into flour and this is the basis for the various types of mustard. The different textures result from differences in the severity of the grinding, and the differences in taste are primarily the result of use of different ingredients in addition to the mustard itself.
Nam Pla	A Thai flavoring sauce made from fermented fish. The ancient Romans made a similar sauce called Garum. Buy Nam Pla at your local oriental market. May also be in the International Section in your supermarket.
Non-reactive	pans made from materials other than aluminum or copper. These latter materials will react with acids, such as tomatoes, vinegar and lemon.
Olive Oil	According to the International Olive Oil Council, there are grades of olive oil: Extra Virgin, Virgin and Pure. Extra Virgin olive oil is the first cold pressing of olives. Virgin olive oil is a flavorful blend of Extra Virgin and Pure olive oil. Pure olive oil is from the second and/or third pressing. Extra Virgin is the best for eating on salads and in any food in which an olive oil flavor is important. Virgin and Pure are more economical for cooking.

Onions	Onions, chives, green onions, leeks, and shallots are members of the allium family, as is garlic. Common onions have been cultivated since Biblical times. Because of it's decided taste, onion is used more as a flavoring agent than as a vegetable. Green, or spring onions are immature onions and are milder in flavor than mature onions. Shallots are smaller and firmer than onions, and are more often used cooked than raw. Chives are more often used as garnish, especially their green parts and flowers. Leeks were developed in ancient Egypt and are used as a vegetable rather than as a flavoring. Leeks are a symbol of the Welsh.
Pad Thai	A Thai dish whose principal ingredients are rice needles, egg, tofu, and shrimp. See the recipe in the Pasta Chapter
Pan spray	No-stick cooking spray made from vegetable oil, such as "Pam".
Parmesan	A hard dry Italian cheese. Usually grated or shredded.
Parmigiana	A method of preparation which involves use of Parmesan cheese. See Green Bean Parmigiana recipe in Vegetable Chapter.
Pasta	The best Italian pasta is made from hard durum wheat because it absorbs less water as it cooks than that made from other wheat. Most familiar pastas are sold dry in packages and are made from simple flour and water dough. Among these are macaroni, spaghetti, lasagna and all the pasta shapes, such as penne.

The other dough is made with eggs and flour. The best known are tortellini and fettucine.

Chinese noodles (pasta also) in addition to being made from wheat, are also made from a host of other starches, such as rice.

Pastry Types   See Pâté au Choux, patty shells, puff pastry, Pâté Brisée and Phyllo dough.

Pâté au Choux   This is the French word used for the dough made into cream puff shells and eclairs. The word literally means cabbage pastry because the knobby look of the cream puff resembles that of the cabbage. They are easy to make and elegant. Try my recipes.

Pâté Brisée   This is simply pie pastry. It's not difficult to make, but with frozen pie shells so readily available and so good, why bother?

Patty Shells   Patty shells are pastry shells made from puff paste dough, sold in supermarkets in the frozen food case. The puff paste dough itself is also available for making puff pastry "pie shells" and other shapes. Patty shells are used in main dishes, such as the Vol au Vent dishes in this book, and in desserts of various kinds. Don't even try to make the dough yourself, you have much better uses for your time. Buy it!

Pepper Capsicums: Bell (sweet) peppers, paprika, and hot or chilli peppers are members of the capsicum annum family and are native to Central and South America. Columbus was searching for pepper (piper nigum) and hot chillies were as close as he could come. He took chillies back to Europe with him.

Pepper:	Pepper is a climbing bush, and is native to India, but now is cultivated widely in tropical areas. Both black and white pepper come from peppercorns. Black pepper is made from unripe or green peppercorns which are sun-dried. The sun-drying gives them their black and wrinkled appearance. White pepper is made from ripe peppercorns from which the outer cover is removed. Green pepper is made from unripe peppercorns preserved in brine. Hint: I have noticed that black pepper has a tendency to intensify in strength when it is in a dish which is reheated. Cayenne, which is made from dried chilli peppers seems more stable.
Pesto, Basil	A paste made of olive oil, basil, pine nuts or walnuts and Parmesan cheese.
Phyllo Dough	This is a Middle Eastern pastry dough that is very difficult to make and tricky to handle. Fortunately you can buy it refrigerated or frozen. Do so, and follow the label directions.
Pistou	A soup flavored with pesto.
Po Boy	A traditional New Orleans sandwich consisting of French bread and some, generally hot, filling. The most popular Po Boy is hot roast beef, with gravy, lettuce and tomatoes. Other popular Po Boys include hot fried shrimp, fish or oysters. Oyster Po Boys are also called Oyster Loaf, or half loaf, depending on the size of the bread.
Poivre Vert	Literally means green pepper. It is a kind of cream sauce made from green peppercorns, to be used with meat.

Simply Delicious by Orva

Polenta	A dish usually made from corn meal. See the recipe in the Breads and Such Chapter.
Pric Nam Pla	A peppery hot version of Nam Pla (fish sauce). See the recipe in the Dressings and Sauces Chapter of this book. See also "Nam Pla".
Provençal	Literally, as in the provinces. Generally refers to dishes made with a characteristic light French tomato sauce.
Puff Paste	A kind of dough made specifically to produce a multilayered flaky pastry used in patty shells or Vol au Vent shells. It is also called "mille feuille", which means literally "a thousand leaves". It is difficult and time consuming to make and easy to find in your grocer's frozen food case. See also "patty shells".
Purée	The dictionary defines this as food made into a pulp, by boiling. Other ways include processing in a food processor, or a blender.
Quiche	A savory pie of custard, usually with cheese and other ingredients such as ham, or bacon, or onions etc.
Rice	There are many varieties of rice, which is second only to wheat in importance as a food grain. Rice may be divided into three main types: long, medium and short grain. White rice has had the husk or bran removed, while brown rice retains the bran, and is more nutritious and nuttier tasting. Parboiled or converted rice has been steamed and then dried prior to packaging. It has the advantage of being less starchy and therefore less sticky when cooked. Wild rice isn't rice at all, but is a freshwater grass and is native to North America.

Rouille	A thick mayonnaise and garlic mixture to be dolloped into soup at table. It adds flavor and a creamy richness. See the recipe for Easy Rouille in the Dressings and Sauces Chapter of this book.
Roux	A brown paste made of equal parts flour and some shortening such as vegetable oil, butter or meat drippings. It is produced by putting flour into the hot fat and gently browning the mixture over a rather low flame. It is then used to thicken and flavor the gravy or sauces, without producing lumps. A flour-fat mixture is readily absorbed by hot liquid; whereas, flour alone, or flour and water form lumps.
Saga Blue	One of the many varieties of veined (or blue) cheeses. It is from Denmark, and is a triple cream blue Brie. Some other Varieties of Blue cheeses are: Roqufort, Danish Blue, Gorganzola, Stilton.
Saltimbocca	The word means "jump in the mouth". It is a way to prepare food that is quick to the table. Try my recipe for Pork Cutlets Saltimbocca.
Sauce	A liquid collection of ingredients, to be poured over food. Often the liquid is the juices of the food itself. If thickened I usually refer to it as gravy. See "gravy".
Sauté	To place food in a skillet with a layer of hot oil or fat, and to cook it, turning as necessary to brown all sides. See "fry".
Schnitzel	A cutlet usually breaded and sautéed. Try one of the schnitzel recipes in this book.

Shepherd's Pie	A lamb pie topped with mashed potatoes rather than a crust. See also "cottage pie".
Simmer	To boil gently, or just be on the point of boiling.
Snail Butter	The type of garlic butter that is used for the preparation of snails. It is used in this book to sauté shrimp.
Sour Cream	Cream which has been caused to sour by the addition of a bacteria culture or by the addition of vinegar.
Spaetzele	A thick noodle, Germanic in origin. Try the Pork Schnitzel with Spaetzele in the Pork Chapter of this book.
Sweet Potatoes	Sweet potatoes are in no way related to white potatoes. Sweet potatoes are members of the Ipomoea family as are morning glories. They are a native of Central and South America and were taken back to Europe by Columbus. As the term "yam" is used in America, it means the orange fleshed sweet potato. White or yellow sweet potatoes are simply called sweet potatoes. The real yam is another vegetable entirely and is native to Africa and Asia. Thus, "yams" and sweet potatoes found in American markets can be used interchangeably.
Tenderize	In this book I suggest that you ask your butcher to "tenderize" a cutlet or some other cut. This is a process in which the meat is pounded with mallet designed to make many deep impressions in the meat, or put through a machine that has the same effect, to flatten and tenderize a chop.
Vinaigrette	A very simple salad dressing of Oil and Vinegar.

See the recipe in the Dressings and Sauces Chapter in this book.

Vol au Vent   A puff pastry shell. See "patty shells".

Index

A

Almonds
　Green Beans Amandine 178
　Sautéed Red Bliss Potatoes with Almonds 177
Amandine
　Information 277
Apple(s)
　Apple and Prune Clafouti 223
　Apple Crisp 219
　Apple Puff 243
　Apple Sauce 220
　Baked Apples with Blackberry Jam 234
　Blueberry and Apple Charlotte 230
　Fried Apples 220
　Plum and Apple Cobbler 231

Apricots
　A Compote Of Strawberries And Apricots 218
　Apricot Tart 253
Arrabbiata
　Arrabbiata Sauce 156, 190
　Information 277
Artichoke
　Tuna and Artichoke Pie 127
Asparagus
　Creamy Asparagus Soup 13
　Ham and Asparagus Bread Pudding 86
　Pasta with Asparagus and Snail Butter 150
　Pasta with Ham and Asparagus 149
　Warm Chicken and Asparagus Salad 40

Avocado
    Avocado and Orange Salad 37

B

Balsamic Vinegar
    Balsamic Vinaigrette Dressing 183
    Information 277
Banana
    Banana and Toffee Fool 213
    Banana Cheesecake Tart 255
    Banana Gingerbread 236
    Banana Pudding 262
    Banana Shortcake 270
    Fruit Salad 216
    Praline Bananas 232
    Tropical Ice Cream 275
Basil
    Basil Vinaigrette 21
    Pesto 5
Béchamel
    Béchamel Sauce 192
    Information 277
Beef 47
    Beef and Oyster Pie 53
    Beef and Pasta Sauté 52
    Beef and Saga Blue Pasta 157
    Beef Bolognese 59
    Beef Curry 70
    Beef Pie 51
    Beef Stroganoff 56
    Beef with Mushrooms 68
    Beef with Saga Blue and Potatoes 71
    Bookmaker Sandwich 73
    Cottage Pie 54
    Country Beef Pie 72
    Creamed Chipped Beef in Vol au Vent Shells 65
    Filet BLT 74
    Garlic and Ginger Beef with Coconut Rice 67
    Grillades and Grits 60
    Hash Gratin 63
    New Orleans Roast Beef 61
    Pasta with Beef and Mushrooms 158
    Pasta with Roast Beef Sauce 62
    Pot Roast with Red Wine 49
    Roast Beef and Tortellini Salad 39
    Roast Beef Hash 63
    Roast Beef Po Boy 62
    Roast Beef Salad 29
    Sauerbraten and Dumplings 57
    Sautéed Filets Poivre Vert 66
    Sesame Beef 70
    Steak Sandwiches Sublime 64
Beets
    Beet Salad with Oranges and Walnuts 28
    Spiced Beet Salad 29
Biscuits
    Black Pepper Biscuits 200
    Buttermilk Biscuits 199
    Sticky Biscuits 225

Black Bean
   Cuban Black Bean and Rice Salad 44
Blackberries
   Baked Apples with Blackberry Jam 234
Blanch
   Information 277
   to blanch vegetables 27
Blueberries
   All American Dessert 211
   Blueberry and Apple Charlotte 230
   Blueberry Bread 228
   Blueberry Cheesecake 271
   Blueberry Crumble Pudding 262
   Blueberry Muffins 229
   Blueberry Peach Crumble 224
   Blueberry Sauce 242, 257
   Lemon Blueberry Pie 246
Braised Cabbage 173
Bread Pudding
   Ham and Asparagus Bread Pudding 86
   Mama's Bread Pudding 261
Breads and Such 197
   Black Pepper Biscuits 200
   Buttermilk Biscuits 199
   Cornbread 203
   Basic Cornbread Dressing 121, 202
   Cheese and Corn Cornbread 204
   Cheese Cornbread 203
   Dumplings 201
   Irish Soda Bread 206
   Irish Soda Bread with Cheese and Walnuts 207
   Patty Cakes 204
   Polenta 206
   Southern Dumplings 201
   Spaetzele 205
Broth
   chicken 3
Brownie Cobbler 228
Bruschetta
   Information 277
Buerre Manie 102
   Information 277
Buttermilk
   Information 277
   Butternut Squash Parmesan 170

C

Cabbage
   Braised Cabbage 173
   Curried Cabbage 169
   overcooking 172
   Quick Sweet and Sour Cabbage 165
   Sweet and Sour Cabbage with Orange or Tangerine 174
Cacciatora
   Information 278
   Quick Cacciatora 102
Caesar Salad Dressing 42, 186
Cake
   Banana Shortcake 270
   Chocolate Cake 273
   Chocolate Walnut Cake 268

Mango Meringue Cake 268
Mango Upside-Down Cake 269
Snow White and Rose Red 272
Very Chocolate Cake 273
Cantaloupe
Blushing Fruit Salad 217
Summertime Dessert 218
Charlotte
Blueberry and Apple Charlotte 230
Cheese
Baked Macaroni and Cheese 141
Banana Cheesecake Tart 255
Blueberry Cheesecake 271
Cheese and Corn Cornbread 204
Cheese Cornbread 203
Cheesecake New York Style 265
Cheesecake Strawberry Pie 252
Chili Con Queso 139
Grilled Swiss Cheese on Sourdough or Rye Bread 143
Irish Soda Bread with Cheese and Walnuts 207
Quiche with Bacon, Cheese and Green Onion 144
Quick Cheese Cakes 272
Stacked Cheese Enchiladas 139
Strawberries with Ricotta 213
Topping for Cheese Cake 266
Chicken
Breast of Chicken "Cordon Bleu" 104
Breast of Chicken Stuffed with Stilton 113
Chicken and Dumpling Soup 11
Chicken and Eggplant Pasta 154
Chicken and Spaghetti 118
Chicken Breast with Shallots 107
Chicken Salad with Bacon 30
Chicken Salad with Pineapple Dressing 41
Chicken Tenders with Stroganoff Sauce 111
Chicken with Oysters 112
Chicken with Southern Dumplings 100
Curried Chicken 116
Curried Chicken Salad 22
Dijon Chicken 105
Easy Repeats 110
Lime Fried Chicken 117
Paprika Chicken 114
Pesto Chicken 110
Poulet Mistral 107
Quick Cacciatora 102
Sautéed Goujonettes of Chicken Breast 99
Warm Chicken and Asparagus Salad 40
Chicken Tenders
Information 278

Chili
    Turkey Chili 122
Chipped Beef
    Creamed Chipped Beef in Vol au Vent Shells 65
Chocolate
    Baked Chocolate Filled Pears with Custard 258
    Chocolate Cake 273
    Chocolate Fondue 237
    Chocolate Ganache Frosting 274
    Chocolate Pie Ice Cream 275
    Chocolate Walnut Cake 268
    Very Chocolate Cake 273
    Chocolate Pie 244
Chop
    Information 278
Chorizo
    Tex-Mex Frittata 93
Chowder 4
Clafouti
    Apple and Prune Clafouti 223
    Mango Clafouti 227
Cobbler
    Georgia Peach Cobbler 222
    Information 278
    Peach and Pineapple Cobbler 235
    Plum and Apple Cobbler 231
Cobbles
    Information 278
Coconut
    Caramelized Pineapple with Coconut Custard 263
    Coconut Custard 263
    Coconut Macaroons 267
    Coconut Rice 68, 176
    Southern Ambrosia 212
    Tropical Ice Cream 275
Cole Slaw 24
    Cole Slaw Bowl 31
Compote
    A Compote Of Strawberries And Apricots 218
    Orange Compote 215
Cordon Bleu
    Breast of Chicken "Cordon Bleu" 104
    Information 278
    Pork Cutlets "Cordon Bleu" 91
Corn
    Corn Chowder 4
    Southern "Fried" Corn 178
    Cornbread 203
    Basic Cornbread Dressing 121, 202
Cottage Pie
    Information 278
    Country Gravy 194
Cranberry
    Fancied-up Cranberry Sauce 120, 191
Cream
    Information 278
Crisp
    Apple Crisp 219
Crumble
    Blueberry Crumble Pudding 262
    Blueberry Peach Crumble 224

Crustades
 Information 279
Cucumber
 Cucumber and Tomato Salad with Basil Vinaigrette 21
 Cumberland Sauce 193
Curd
 Lemon Curd 242, 257
Curry(ied)
 Beef Curry 70
 Curried Cabbage 169
 Curried Chicken 116
 Curried Chicken Salad 22
 Curried Pumpkin Soup 8
 Curried Rice Salad 24
Custard
 Caramelized Pineapple with Coconut Custard 263
 Coconut Custard 263
 Lemon Custard Pudding 259
Cutlet
 Information 279

D

Deglazing 59
 Information 279
Desserts 209
  A Compote Of Strawberries And Apricots 218
  All American Dessert 211
  Apple and Prune Clafouti 223
  Apple Crisp 219
  Apple Puff 243
  Apple Sauce 220

Apricot Tart 253
Baked Apples with Blackberry Jam 234
Baked Chocolate Filled Pears with Custard 258
Banana and Toffee Fool 213
Banana Cheesecake Tart 255
Banana Gingerbread 236
Banana Pudding 262
Banana Shortcake 270
Blonde Mincemeat 232
Blueberry and Apple Charlotte 230
Blueberry Bread 228
Blueberry Cheesecake 271
Blueberry Crumble Pudding 262
Blueberry Muffins 229
Blueberry Peach Crumble 224
Blueberry Sauce 242, 257
Blushing Fruit Salad 217
Brownie Cobbler 228
Caramelized Pineapple with Coconut Custard 263
Cheesecake New York Style 265
Cheesecake Strawberry Pie 252
Chocolate Cake 273
Chocolate Fondue 237
Chocolate Ganache Frosting 274
Chocolate Pie 244
Chocolate Pie Ice Cream 275

Chocolate Walnut Cake 268
Coconut Custard 263
Coconut Macaroons 267
Dessert, Quick and Easy 214
Dulce de Leche Tart 254
French Pear Pie 240
Fried Apples 220
Fruit Salad 216
Fruit Salad Dressing 215
Georgia Peach Cobbler 222
Lemon Blueberry Pie 246
Lemon Curd 242, 257
Lemon Custard Pudding 259
Lemon "Pseudo" Ice Box Pie 243
Luscious Lemon Pie 239
Mama's Bread Pudding 261
Mango Clafouti 227
Mango Meringue Cake 268
Mango, Strawberry Sundae 276
Mango Upside-Down Cake 269
Marlboro Pie 241
Meringues 244
Orange Compote 215
Peach and Pineapple Cobbler 235
Pear and Mincemeat Flan 250
Pecan Pie 248
Pineapple Puff 253
Pineapple Tarts 251
Plantains for Dessert 233
Plum and Apple Cobbler 231
Pousse Café Tart 241
Praline Bananas 232
Profiteroles (Cream Puffs) 221
Quick Cheese Cakes 272
Rubble 247
Snow White and Rose Red 272
Southern Ambrosia 212
Special Peach Pie 237
Sticky Biscuits 225
Strawberries with Ricotta 213
Strawberry Fool 211
Strawberry Meringue 245
Strawberry Short Mousse 264
Summertime Dessert 218
Topping for Cheese Cake 266
Tropical Ice Cream 275
Upside Down Ginger Pear Cake 266
Upside Down Pudding 256
Very Chocolate Cake 273
Walnut Tart (Flan) 249
Whipped Cream 214
Zippy Peach Pudding 260

Dice
    Information 279
Dijon Mustard
    Dijon and Garlic Salad Dressing 37, 185
    Dijon Chicken 105
Dressing 181
    Basic Cornbread Dressing 121
    Fruit Salad Dressing 215

Information 279
Dulce de Leche
  Dulce de Leche Tart 254
  Information 279
Dumplings
  Chicken and Dumpling Soup 11
  Chicken with Southern Dumplings 100
  Dumplings 201
  Information 280
  Sauerbraten and Dumplings 57
  Southern Dumplings 101, 201

E

Eggplant
  Chicken and Eggplant Pasta 154
  Eggplant and Pasta Gratin 155
  Eggplant 'Napoleons' 167
  Pasta with Eggplant and Tomato 153
Eggs
  Beating Eggs 78
  Ham and Egg Cobbler 82
Eggs and Cheese 137
  Baked Macaroni and Cheese 141
  Chili Con Queso 139
  Goldenrod Eggs 140
  Grilled Swiss Cheese on Sourdough or Rye Bread 143
  Quiche with Bacon, Cheese and Green Onion 144
  Shrimp Egg Foo Yong 142
  Stacked Cheese Enchiladas 139
Enchiladas
  Stacked Cheese Enchiladas 139
Evaporated Milk
  Information 280

F

Feta Cheese
  Tomato Salad with Feta 45
Fettucini
  Fettucini with Fresh Tomato Sauce and Bacon 162
Fish
  Soupe De Poisson Rapide 10
Flour
  Information 280
Fondue
  Chocolate Fondue 237
Fool
  Banana and Toffee Fool 213
  Information 280
  Strawberry Fool 211
Fresh Tomato Sauce 188
Frosting
  Chocolate Ganache Frosting 274
Fruit Salad 216
  Fruit Salad Dressing 215
Fry
  Information 280

G

Garlic
  Information 281
Gazpacho 3
Ginger
  Garlic and Ginger Beef with Coconut Rice 67
  selecting 67
Gingerbread
  Banana Gingerbread 236
Glaze
  Baked Ham with Bourbon and Sugar Glaze 77
Goujonettes
  Information 281
  Sautéed Goujonettes of Chicken Breast 99
Gratin
  Eggplant and Pasta Gratin 155
  Ham and Cheese Gratin 79
  Hash Gratin 63
  Information 281
  Mirleton Gratin 171
Gravy
  Country Gravy 90, 194
  Information 281
  Turkey Gravy 120, 191
Green Beans
  Green Beans Amandine 178
  Green Beans Parmigiana 169
  Green Peas
  Pasta with Green Peas and Salmon 160
Green Peppercorn(s)
  Green Peppercorn Salad Dressing 34, 184
  Sautéed Filets Poivre Vert 66
  Steak Salad With Green Peppercorn Dressing 33
Grillades and Grits 60
  Grits 175
Gumbo 6

H

Ham
  Baked Ham with Bourbon and Brown Sugar Glaze 77
  Country Ham 78
  fully cooked 78
  Ham and Asparagus Bread Pudding 86
  Ham and Cheese Gratin 79
  Ham and Cheese Rolls 81
  Ham and Egg Cobbler 82
  Pasta with Ham and Asparagus 149
  Pasta with Ham and Spinach 147
  Sweet Potato and Ham Medley 85
Ham Glaze
  Information 281
Hash
  Roast Beef Hash 63
Hot Sauce
  Information 281

I

Ice Cream

Chocolate Pie Ice Cream 275
Tropical Ice Cream 275
Irish Soda Bread 206
   Irish Soda Bread with Cheese and Walnuts 207
Italian Sausage
   Pasta with Hot Italian Sausage 156
   Pasta with Hot Italian Sausage and Winter Squash 159
   Special Italian Sausage 93

K

Kale
   Cooked Fresh Kale 174
Kedgeree
   Information 282
   Salmon Kedgeree 131

L

Leftovers
   Chicken
   Chicken Salad with Bacon 30
   Chicken Vol au Vent 109
   Chicken with Southern Dumplings 100
   Easy Repeats 110
   Quick Cacciatora 102
   Ham
   Ham and Asparagus Bread Pudding 86
   Ham and Cheese Gratin 79
   Ham and Cheese Rolls 81
   Ham and Egg Cobbler 82

Sweet Potato and Ham Medley 85
Roast Beef
   Beef Pie 51
   Country Beef Pie 72
   Hash Gratin 63
   Pasta with Roast Beef Sauce 62
   Roast Beef and Tortellini Salad 39
   Roast Beef Hash 63
   Roast Beef Po Boy 62
   Roast Beef Salad 29
Lemon
   Lemon Blueberry Pie 246
   Lemon Curd 242, 257
   Lemon Custard Pudding 259
   Lemon "Pseudo" Ice Box Pie 243
   Luscious Lemon Pie 239
Light Tomato Sauce 188
Lime
   Lime Fried Chicken 117

M

Macaroni
   Baked Macaroni and Cheese 141
   French Bistro Macaroni 151
Macaroons
   Coconut Macaroons 267
Mango
   Mango Clafouti 227
   Mango Meringue Cake 268
   Mango Sauce 45, 186

Mango, Strawberry Sundae 276
Mango Upside-Down Cake 269
Tropical Ice Cream 275
Marchand de Vin
    Information 282
    Marchand de Vin Sauce 187
Marinate
    Information 282
Marlboro Pie 241
Mashed Potatoes 170
Mayonnaise 9
Meringue
    Making Meringues 244
    Mango Meringue Cake 268
    Strawberry Meringue 245
Mincemeat
    Blonde Mincemeat 232
    Pear and Mincemeat Flan 250
Mirleton
    Information 282
    Mirleton Gratin 171
Mistral
    Information 282
Mousse
    Strawberry Short Mousse 264
Muffins
    Blueberry Muffins 229
Mushroom(s)
    Beef with Mushrooms 68
    Mushroom and Garlic Soup 14
    Pasta with Beef and Mushrooms 158
    selecting 15

Mustard
    Information 282

N

Nam Pla
    Information 283
Non-reactive
    Information 283

O

Okra
    Gumbo 6
Olive Oil
    Information 283
Onions
    Information 283
Orange(s)
    Avocado and Orange Salad 37
    Beet Salad with Oranges and Walnuts 28
    Dessert, Quick and Easy 214
    Orange Compote 215
    Southern Ambrosia 212
    Sweet and Sour Cabbage with Orange or Tangerine 174
Oyster
    Beef and Oyster Pie 53
    Chicken with Oysters 112

P

Pad Thai 160
    Information 284
Pan spray
    Information 284

Paprika
   Paprika Chicken 114
Parmesan
   Butternut Squash Parmesan 170
   Information 284
   Pumpkin with Parmesan 173
Parmigiana
   Green Beans Parmigiana 169
   Information 284
Pasta 145
   Beef and Pasta Sauté 52
   Beef and Saga Blue Pasta 157
   Chicken and Eggplant Pasta 154
   Eggplant and Pasta Gratin 155
   Fettucini with Fresh Tomato Sauce and Bacon 162
   French Bistro Macaroni 151
   Information 284
   Lemon and Butter Pasta 152
   Pad Thai 160
   Pasta with Asparagus and Snail Butter 150
   Pasta with Beef and Mushrooms 158
   Pasta with Creamy Sauce 148
   Pasta with Eggplant and Tomato 153
   Pasta with Green Peas and Salmon 160
   Pasta with Ham and Asparagus 149
   Pasta with Ham and Spinach 147
   Pasta with Hot Italian Sausage 156
   Pasta with Hot Italian Sausage and Winter Squash 159
   Pasta with Roast Beef Sauce 62
Pastry Type
   Information 284
   Pâté au Choux
      Information 284
   Pâté Brisée
      Information 284
   Patty Cakes 204
   Patty Shells
      Information 285
   Pavé 66
Peach(es)
   Blueberry Peach Crumble 224
   Georgia Peach Cobbler 222
   Peach and Pineapple Cobbler 235
   Special Peach Pie 237
   Zippy Peach Pudding 260
Pear(s)
   Baked Chocolate Filled Pears with Custard 258
   French Pear Pie 240
   Pear and Mincemeat Flan 250
   Upside Down Ginger Pear Cake 266
Peas
   Creamed Peas and New Potatoes 172
Pecan Pie 248

Pepper(s)
   Information 285
   to roast 27
Peppercorn(s)
   Green Peppercorn Salad Dressing 34, 184
   Sautéed Filets Poivre Vert 66
   Steak Salad With Green Peppercorn Dressing 33
Pesto 5
   Information 285
   Pesto Chicken 110
Phyllo Dough
   Information 285
Pie Crust 248
Pie, Savory
   Beef and Oyster Pie 53
   Beef Pie 51
   Cottage Pie 54
   Tuna and Artichoke Pie 127
Pie, Sweet
   Apple Puff 243
   Apricot Tart 253
   Banana Cheesecake Tart 255
   Blueberry Cheesecake 271
   Cheesecake Strawberry Pie 252
   Chocolate Pie 244
   Dulce de Leche Tart 254
   French Pear Pie 240
   Lemon Blueberry Pie 246
   Lemon "Pseudo" Ice Box Pie 243
   Luscious Lemon Pie 239
   Marlboro Pie 241
   Pear and Mincemeat Flan 250
   Pecan Pie 248
   Pineapple Puff 253
   Pineapple Tarts 251
   Pousse Café Tart 241
   Quick Cheese Cakes 272
   Special Peach Pie 237
   Topping for Cheese Cake 266
   Walnut Tart (Flan) 249
Pineapple
   Caramelized Pineapple with Coconut Custard 263
   Chicken Salad with Pineapple Dressing 41
   Dessert, Quick and Easy 214
   Fruit Salad 216
   Peach and Pineapple Cobbler 235
   Pineapple Puff 253
   Pineapple Tarts 251
Pistou
   Information 286
Plantain
   Plantains for Dessert 233
Plum(s)
   Plum and Apple Cobbler 231
Po Boy
   Information 286
   Roast Beef Po Boy 62
   Sausage Po Boy 92
Poivre Vert
   Information 286
Polenta 206
   Information 286
Pork 75

Baked Ham with Bourbon and Brown Sugar Glaze 77
Ham and Asparagus Bread Pudding 86
Ham and Cheese Gratin 79
Ham and Cheese Rolls 81
Ham and Egg Cobbler 82
Oriental Pork Burgers 87
Pork Country Fried Steak 89
Pork Cutlets "Cordon Bleu" 91
Pork Cutlets Saltimbocca 94
Pork Schnitzel 83
Pork Schnitzel With Shallot And Tomato Sauce 95
Roast Pork Mistral 88
Sausage Po Boy 92
Sautéed Pork Chops 80
Special Italian Sausage 93
Sweet Potato and Ham Medley 85
Tex-Mex Frittata 93
Pot Roast
   Pot Roast with Red Wine 49
Potato(es)
   Beef with Saga Blue and Potatoes 71
   Creamed Peas and New Potatoes 172
   Mashed Potatoes 170
   Potato Salad 34
   Potato Salad with Bacon 35
   Roasted Potato Salad with Dijon and Garlic Dressing 36
   Sautéed Potatoes with Rosemary 166
   Sautéed Red Bliss Potatoes with Almonds 177
Poultry. See Chicken or Turkey
Pousse Café Tart 241
Pric Nam Pla
   Information 286
   Prik Nam Pla 162, 195
Profiteroles (Cream Puffs) 221
Provençal
   Information 286
Prune(s)
   Apple and Prune Clafouti 223
Pudding
   Banana Pudding 262
   Blueberry Crumble Pudding 262
   Lemon Custard Pudding 259
   Mama's Bread Pudding 261
   Upside Down Pudding 256
   Zippy Peach Pudding 260
Puff Paste
   Information 286
Pumpkin
   Curried Pumpkin Soup 8
   Pumpkin with Parmesan 173
Purée
   Information 286

Q

Quiche
   Information 287
   Quiche with Bacon, Cheese and Green Onion 144

R

Raspberries
  Blushing Fruit Salad 217
  Red Bliss 166
Rice
  Coconut Rice 68, 176
  Cuban Black Bean and Rice Salad 44
  Curried Rice Salad 24
  Garlic and Ginger Beef with Coconut Rice 67
  Information 287
  Rice Salad 23
Ricotta
  Strawberries with Ricotta 213
Roast
  Pot Roast with Red Wine 49
  Roast Beef Hash Gratin 63
  New Orleans Roast Beef 61
  Pasta with Roast Beef Sauce 62
  Roast Beef and Tortellini Salad 39
  Roast Beef Hash 63
  Roast Beef Po Boy 62
  Roast Beef Salad 29
Rouille 11
  Easy Rouille 194
  Information 287
Roux 7
  Information 287
Rubble 247

S

Saga Blue
  Beef and Saga Blue Pasta 157
  Beef with Saga Blue and Potatoes 71
  Information 287
Salad 19
  Avocado and Orange Salad 37
  Beet Salad with Oranges and Walnuts 28
  Caesar Salad 42
  Caribbean Shrimp Salad 44
  Chicken Salad with Bacon 30
  Chicken Salad with Pineapple Dressing 41
  Cole Slaw 24
  Cole Slaw Bowl 31
  Cuban Black Bean and Rice Salad 44
  Cucumber and Tomato with Basil Vinaigrette 21
  Curried Chicken 22
  Curried Rice Salad 24
  Green Salad with Bacon 25
  Not-Your-Usual Three Bean Salad 27
  Potato Salad 34
  Potato Salad with Bacon 35
  Rice Salad 23
  Roast Beef and Tortellini Salad 39
  Roast Beef Salad 29
  Roasted Potato Salad with Dijon and Garlic Dressing 36

Salmon Salad   38
Salsa   25
Spanish Salad   26
Spiced Beet Salad   29
Steak Salad With Green Peppercorn Dressing   33
Three Vegetable Salad with Balsamic Vinaigrette   43
Tomato Salad with Feta   45
Tuna Salad   32
Vegetable Salad   32
Warm Chicken and Asparagus Salad   40
Salad Dressing
  Balsamic Dressing   185
  Balsamic Vinaigrette Dressing   183
  Basil Vinaigrette   21
  Blue Cheese Dressing   30
  Caesar Salad Dressing   42, 186
  Creamy Tomato Dressing   39, 184
  Dijon and Garlic Dressing   37, 185
  for Curried Chicken Salad   22
  for Rice Salad   23
  Fruit Salad Dressing   215
  Green Peppercorn Salad Dressing   34, 184
  Mango Sauce   45
  Vinaigrette Dressing   26, 183
Salmon
  Pasta with Green Peas and Salmon   160
  Salmon Kedgeree   131
  Salmon Nuggets   128
  Salmon Salad   38
  Simply Delicious Salmon Cakes   129
Salsa
  Salad   25
Saltimbocca
  Information   288
Sandwich
  Bookmaker Sandwich   73
  Filet BLT   74
  Grilled Swiss Cheese on Sourdough or Rye Bread   143
  Ham and Cheese Rolls   81
  Sausage Po Boy   92
  Steak Sandwiches Sublime   64
Sauce   181
  Arrabbiata Sauce   156, 190
  Béchamel Sauce   192
  Blueberry Sauce   242, 257
  Country Gravy   90, 194
  Cumberland Sauce   193
  Easy Rouille   194
  Egg Foo Yong Sauce   143
  Fancied-up Cranberry Sauce   120, 191
  Fresh Tomato Sauce   103, 188
  Information   288
  Light Tomato Sauce   102, 188
  Mango Sauce   186
  Marchand de Vin Sauce   187
  Prik Nam Pla   162, 195
  Quick Tomato Sauce   189

Shallot And Tomato Sauce 96, 189
Snail Butter 135, 193
Turkey Gravy 120, 191
White Sauce with Cheese 140
Sauerbraten
Sauerbraten and Dumplings 57
Sausage
  Pasta with Hot Italian Sausage 156
  Pasta with Hot Italian Sausage and Winter Squash 159
  Sausage Po Boy 92
  Special Italian Sausage 93
  Tex-Mex Frittata 93
Sauté
  Information 288
Schnitzel
  Information 288
  Pork Schnitzel 83
  Pork Schnitzel With Shallot And Tomato Sauce 95
Seafood 125
  Beef and Oyster Pie 53
  Charleston Shrimp 136
  Dinner Bruschetta 130
  Pasta with Green Peas and Salmon 160
  Pesto Prawns 133
  Salmon Kedgeree 131
  Salmon Nuggets 128
  Shrimp Aurora 134
  Shrimp Egg Foo Yong 142
  Shrimp Provençal 132
  Shrimps with Snail Butter 135

Simply Delicious Salmon Cakes 129
Soupe De Poisson Rapide 10
Tuna and Artichoke Pie 127
Shepherd's Pie
  Information 288
Shortcake
  Banana Shortcake 270
  Strawberry Short Mousse 264
Shrimp
  Caribbean Shrimp Salad 44
  Charleston Shrimp 136
  Gumbo 6
  Pesto Prawns 133
  Shrimp Aurora 134
  Shrimp Egg Foo Yong 142
  Shrimp Provençal 132
  Shrimps with Snail Butter 135
Simmer
  Information 288
Snail Butter 135, 193
  Information 288
  Pasta with Asparagus and Snail Butter 150
  Shrimps with Snail Butter 135
Soda Bread, Irish 206
  Irish Soda Bread with Cheese and Walnuts 207
Soup 1
  broth 3
  Chicken and Dumpling 11
  Corn Chowder 4
  Creamy Asparagus 13
  Creamy French Celery 12

Creamy Tomato 5
Curried Pumpkin 8
Gazpacho 3
Minestrone Rapide 16
Mushroom and Garlic 14
Pistou 17
Quick Shrimp Gumbo 6
Soupe De Poisson Rapide 10
stock 3
Sour Cream
   Information 288
Spaetzele 84, 205
   Information 288
Spaghetti
   Chicken and Spaghetti 118
Spinach
   Pasta with Ham and Spinach 147
Squash
   Butternut Squash Parmesan 170
   Pasta with Hot Italian Sausage and Winter Squash 159
   Sautéed Summer Squash with Onion 179
Steak
   Steak Sandwiches Sublime 64
Sticky Biscuits 225
Stilton
   Breast of Chicken Stuffed with Stilton 113
   Stock 3
Strawberries
   A Compote Of Strawberries And Apricots 218
   All American Dessert 211
   Cheesecake Strawberry Pie 252
   Fruit Salad 216
   Mango, Strawberry Sundae 276
   Rubble 247
   Snow White and Rose Red 272
   Strawberries with Ricotta 213
   Strawberry Fool 211
   Strawberry Meringue 245
   Strawberry Short Mousse 264
   Summertime Dessert 218
Stroganoff
   Beef Stroganoff 56
   Chicken Tenders with Stroganoff Sauce 111
Sunday
   Mango, Strawberry Sundae 276
Sweet and Sour Cabbage
   Quick Sweet and Sour Cabbage 165
   Sweet and Sour Cabbage with Orange or Tangerine 174
Sweet Potato(es)
   goes with 168
   Information 288
   peeling trick 85
   Savory Sweet Potatoes 168
   Sweet Potato and Ham Medley 85

T

Tangerine
   Sweet and Sour Cabbage with Orange or Tangerine 174
Tenderize Information 289
Tomato
   Arrabbiata Sauce 190
   Creamy Tomato Dressing 184
   Creamy Tomato Salad Dressing 39
   Cucumber and Tomato Salad with Basil Vinaigrette 21
   Fettucini with Fresh Tomato Sauce and Bacon 162
   Fresh Tomato Sauce 103, 188
   Light Tomato Sauce 102, 188
   Pasta with Eggplant and Tomato 153
   Quick Tomato Sauce 189
   Shallot And Tomato Sauce 189
   soup 5
   to skin 26
   Tomato Salad with Feta 45
Tortellini
   Roast Beef and Tortellini Salad 39
Tuna
   Dinner Bruschetta 130
   Tuna and Artichoke Pie 127
   Tuna Salad 32
Turkey
   Fancied-up Cranberry Sauce 120
   Roast Turkey 119
   Turkey Chili 122
   Turkey Gravy 120

U

Upside-Down Cake
   Mango Upside-Down Cake 269
   Upside-Down Ginger Pear Cake 266
   Upside-Down Pudding 256

V

Vegetable(s)
   Braised Cabbage 173
   Butternut Squash Parmesan 170
   Coconut Rice 176
   Cooked Fresh Kale 174
   Creamed Peas and New Potatoes 172
   Curried Cabbage 169
   Eggplant 'Napoleons' 167
   Green Beans Amandine 178
   Green Beans Parmigiana 169
   Grits 175
   Mashed Potatoes 170
   Mirleton Gratin 171
   Pumpkin with Parmesan 173
   Quick Sweet and Sour Cabbage 165

Sautéed Potatoes with Rosemary 166
Sautéed Red Bliss Potatoes with Almonds 177
Sautéed Summer Squash with Onion 179
Savory Sweet Potatoes 168
Southern "Fried" Corn 178
Sweet and Sour Cabbage with Orange or Tangerine 174
Three Vegetable Salad with Balsamic Vinaigrette 43
Vegetable Salad 32

Vinaigrette
Information 289
Vinaigrette Dressing 26, 183

Vol au Vent
Chicken Vol au Vent 109
Creamed Chipped Beef in Vol au Vent Shells 65
Information 290

W

Walnut
Beet Salad with Oranges and Walnuts 28
Chocolate Walnut Cake 268
Walnut Tart (Flan) 249

Whipped Cream 214